Trinidad and Tobago

WORLD BIBLIOGRAPHICAL SERIES

General Editors:
Robert L. Collison (Editor-in-chief)
Sheila R. Herstein
Louis J. Reith
Hans H. Wellisch

VOLUMES IN THE SERIES

1 *Yugoslavia*, John J. Horton
2 *Lebanon*, Shereen Khairallah
3 *Lesotho*, Shelagh M. Willet and David Ambrose
4 *Rhodesia/Zimbabwe*, Oliver B. Pollack and Karen Pollack
5 *Saudi Arabia*, Frank A. Clements
6 *USSR*, Anthony Thompson
7 *South Africa*, Reuben Musiker
8 *Malawi*, Robert B. Boeder
9 *Guatemala*, Woodman B. Franklin
11 *Uganda*, Robert L. Collison
12 *Malaysia*, Ian Brown and Rajeswary Ampalavanar
13 *France*, Frances Chambers
14 *Panama*, Eleanor DeSelms Langstaff
15 *Hungary*, Thomas Kabdebo
16 *USA*, Sheila R. Herstein and Naomi Robbins
17 *Greece*, Richard Clogg and Mary Jo Clogg
18 *New Zealand*, R. F. Grover
19 *Algeria*, Richard I. Lawless
21 *Belize*, Ralph Lee Woodward, Jr.
23 *Luxembourg*, Carlo Hury and Jul Christophory
24 *Swaziland*, Balam Nyeko
25 *Kenya*, Robert L. Collison
26 *India*, Brijen K. Gupta and Datta S. Kharbas
27 *Turkey*, Meral Güçlü
28 *Cyprus*, P. M. Kitromilides and M. L. Evriviades
29 *Oman*, Frank A. Clements
31 *Finland*, J. E. O. Screen
32 *Poland*, Richard C. Lewański
33 *Tunisia*, Allan M. Findlay, Anne M. Findlay and Richard I. Lawless
34 *Scotland*, Eric G. Grant
35 *China*, Peter Cheng
36 *Qatar*, P. T. H. Unwin
37 *Iceland*, John J. Horton
39 *Haiti*, Frances Chambers
40 *Sudan*, M. W. Daly
41 *Vatican City State*, Michael J. Walsh
42 *Iraq*, A. J. Abdulrahman
43 *United Arab Emirates*, Frank A. Clements
44 *Nicaragua*, Ralph Lee Woodward, Jr.
45 *Jamaica*, K. E. Ingram
46 *Australia*, I. Kepars
47 *Morocco*, Anne M. Findlay, Allan M. Findlay and Richard I. Lawless
48 *Mexico*, Naomi Robbins
49 *Bahrain*, P. T. H. Unwin
50 *The Yemens*, G. Rex Smith
51 *Zambia*, Anne M. Bliss, J. A. Rigg
52 *Puerto Rico*, Elena E. Cevallos
53 *Namibia*, Stanley Schoeman and Elna Schoeman
54 *Tanzania*, Colin Darch
55 *Jordan*, Ian J. Seccombe
56 *Kuwait*, Frank A. Clements
57 *Brazil*, Solena V. Bryant
58 *Israel*, Esther M. Snyder (preliminary compilation E. Kreiner)
59 *Romania*, Andrea Deletant and Dennis Deletant
60 *Spain*, Graham J. Shields
61 *Atlantic Ocean*, H. G. R. King
63 *Cameroon*, Mark W. Delancey and Peter J. Schraeder
64 *Malta*, John Richard Thackrah
65 *Thailand*, Michael Watts
66 *Austria*, Denys Salt with the assistance of Arthur Farrand Radley
67 *Norway*, Leland B. Sather
68 *Czechoslovakia*, David Short
69 *Irish Republic*, Michael O. Shannon
70 *Pacific Basin and Oceania*, Gerald W. Fry and Rufino Mauricio
74 *Trinidad and Tobago*, Frances Chambers

VOLUME 74

Trinidad and Tobago

Frances Chambers
Compiler
Edited by Sheila Herstein

CLIO PRESS
OXFORD, ENGLAND · SANTA BARBARA, CALIFORNIA
DENVER, COLORADO

British Library Cataloguing in Publication Data

Chambers, Frances
Trinidad and Tobago.—(World bibliographical series; 74)
1. Trinidad and Tobago—Bibliography
I. Title II. Series
016.97298′3 Z1561.T7

ISBN 1–85109–020–7

Clio Press Ltd.,
55 St. Thomas' Street.
Oxford OX1 1JG, England.

ABC-Clio Information Services.
Riviera Campus, 2040 Alameda Padre Serra.
Santa Barbara, Ca. 93103, USA

Designed by Bernard Crossland
Typeset by Columns Design and Production Services, Reading, England
Printed and bound in Great Britain by
Billing and Sons Ltd., Worcester

THE WORLD BIBLIOGRAPHICAL SERIES

This series will eventually cover every country in the world, each in a separate volume comprising annotated entries on works dealing with its history, geography, economy and politics: and with its people, their culture, customs, religion and social organization. Attention will also be paid to current living conditions – housing, education, newspapers, clothing, etc. – that are all too often ignored in standard bibliographies; and to those particular aspects relevant to individual countries. Each volume seeks to achieve, by use of careful selectivity and critical assessment of the literature, an expression of the country and an appreciation of its nature and national aspirations, to guide the reader towards an understanding of its importance. The keynote of the series is to provide, in a uniform format, an interpretation of each country that will express its culture, its place in the world, and the qualities and background that make it unique.

SERIES EDITORS

Robert L. Collison (Editor-in-chief) is Professor Emeritus, Library and Information Studies, University of California, Los Angeles, and is currently the President of the Society of Indexers. Following the war, he served as Reference Librarian for the City of Westminster and later became Librarian to the BBC. During his fifty years as a professional librarian in England and the USA, he has written more than twenty works on bibliography, librarianship, indexing and related subjects.

Sheila R. Herstein is Reference Librarian and Library Instruction Coordinator at the City College of the City University of New York. She has extensive bibliographic experience and has described her innovations in the field of bibliographic instruction in 'Team teaching and bibliographic instruction'. *The Bookmark*, Autumn 1979. In addition, Doctor Herstein coauthored a basic annotated bibliography in history for Funk & Wagnalls *New encyclopedia*, and for several years reviewed books for *Library Journal*.

Louis J. Reith is librarian with the Franciscan Institute, St. Bonaventure University, New York. He received his PhD from Stanford University, California, and later studied at Eberhard-Karls-Universität, Tübingen. In addition to his activities as a librarian, Dr. Reith is a specialist on 16th-century German history and the Reformation and has published many articles and papers in both German and English. He was also editor of the *American Society for Reformation Research Newsletter*.

Hans H. Wellisch is a Professor at the College of Library and Information Services, University of Maryland, and a member of the American Society of Indexers and the International Federation for Documentation. He is the author of numerous articles and several books on indexing and abstracting, and has also published *Indexing and abstracting: an international bibliography*. He also contributes frequently to *Journal of the American Society for Information Science, Library Quarterly*, and *The Indexer*.

For my niece and nephews,
Holly Banko, Bradley Banko, and Gabriel Silver

Contents

Contents

Contents

Introduction

Trinidad and Tobago is a two-island nation situated ten degrees above the equator off the coast of South America. Trindad is both the largest and the southernmost island in the Lesser Antilles chain. Its nearest neighbour, Venezuela, is located on the South American mainland to the west and south. The Caribbean Sea lies to the north, the Atlantic Ocean to the east. Trinidad's partner island, Tobago, is thirty-two kilometres to northeast.

Trinidad is a small island with an area of 1,864 sq. miles (4,828 sq. km.); Tobago is only 116 sq. miles (300 sq. km). Both islands are striped with mountain ranges. The country's most notable physical feature is the Pitch Lake, the world's largest natural asphalt deposit, located in southwestern Trinidad. The climate is tropical with a dry season lasting from January to May. Bird life is particularly abundant.

Trinidad's history has taken many twists and turns. Sighted by Columbus on his third voyage in 1498, the Arawak-inhabited island was claimed for Spain's New World Empire. However, few Spaniards cared to settle on Trinidad, and the Amerindians were soon decimated. Colonization proceeded so slowly, in fact, that in the 1770s the Spanish government took the unprecedented step of offering incentives to foreign Roman Catholics to settle in Trinidad. With the arrival of a flood of French planters and their African slaves, the island soon was only nominally Spanish and the underlying stratum of its present culture was laid down.

In 1797, an event occurred that determined Trinidad's destiny for more than 150 years. Spain had declared war on Britain in 1796. The following year, British warships sailed into the harbour of Port-of-Spain, and the Spanish governor surrendered the island. Trinidad became part of the British Empire and remained so until it achieved independence in the mid-20th century. British law, tradition, culture, religion, and language were superimposed on the essentially French-African land. Tobago, which may have changed hands more than any other island in the Caribbean, was ceded to Britain in 1814.

The 19th century saw first the end of the slave trade, then the emancipation of the Black slaves who worked on the West Indian plantations. In order to provide agricultural manpower, indentured labourers – mostly from the Indian subcontinent – were brought to Trinidad, weaving yet another exotic strand into the island's population. In 1889, Tobago was joined administratively to Trinidad.

After a brief attempt (1958–62) to unite with other British Caribbean islands in the Federation of the West Indies, Trinidad and Tobago achieved full independence through constitutional arrangements on 31 August 1962, becoming a member state of the Commonwealth of Nations. In 1976, the country adopted a new constitution by which it became a republic. Dr. Eric Williams, whose party, the People's National Movement, had been in the forefront of Trinidad and Tobago's politics since 1956, became prime minister at independence and continued in that office until his death in 1981. George Chambers is the current prime minister and the leader of the People's National Movement.

Independence, of course, did not mean the end of the country's problems. Unemployment and inflation continue to cause concern. As an oil producing country, Trinidad and Tobago received an economic windfall during the oil boom of the 1970s. With the decline of oil prices, however, Trinidad has found it necessary to diversify its economy. How well the country meets this challenge will determine whether its economy remains one of the strongest in the Caribbean region. Neither has independence signalled the end of political turmoil, as was shown dramatically in the demonstrations that took place in the spring of 1970. However, despite these economic and political strains, democratic traditions and the rule of law have remained firmly in place in the nation.

Trinidad and Tobago's culture is one of the most cosmopolitan in the world, unique in the blend of French, British, African, and East Indian traditions and customs found in its everyday life and celebrated in exuberant festivities, the best known of which is Carnival. The island-nation is justly famous as the home of calypso music and the birth place of the steelband. At the same time, Trinidadians have achieved recognition for their intellectual accomplishments. Several – Eric Williams, C. L. R. James, V. S.

Naipaul – have displayed near-Renaissance virtuosity as statesmen, scholars, and writers.

The aim of this bibliography is to bring together a selective list of published literature on Trinidad and Tobago that will aid the general reader, the undergraduate student, and the librarian to locate information on the country. The 641 entries have been grouped into 43 categories. In the historical categories, an attempt has been made to arrange entries chronologically; in the other categories, the most recent items will be found first. Annotations are intended to be informative rather than critical. Both books and journal articles are listed, along with a few government publications; theses and dissertations have not been included.

My thanks go to all those who have aided me in the completion of this book. Most of the material was reviewed at libraries in New York City, in particular at the libraries of New York University, Columbia University, and the City College of New York. The librarians with whom I came into contact while preparing this volume were unfailingly courteous and helpful.

I especially wish to thank Stephen Chambers for his part in this book – for his encouragement, advice, and most of all for the generous contribution of his time to this project.

Frances Chambers
New York City
1986

The Country and Its People

1 **Latin America and Caribbean Contemporary Record.**
Edited by Jack W. Hopkins. New York, London: Holmes & Meier, 1983. vol. 1, 1981-82. 892p. maps. bibliog. annual.

An expertly prepared reference tool that presents thematic essays on topics of special interest as well as reviews of the year's developments in political, social, economic, and foreign affairs for each country of the region. The section on Trinidad and Tobago is on p. 622-35.

2 **Background notes: Trinidad & Tobago.**
Washington, DC: US Department of State, Bureau of Public Affairs, 1982. 4p. maps. (Department of State Publication, no. 8306; Background Notes Series).

A periodically updated publication that profiles Trinidad and Tobago's people, geography, government, political conditions, economy, history, defence, and foreign relations. It includes travel notes and a list of principal government officials.

3 **Tobago.**
David L. Niddrie. Cork, Irish Republic: Litho Press; Gainesville, Florida: Midleton, 1980. 243p. maps. bibliog.

A general, all-round handbook on Tobago, written by an American who first became acquainted with the island while engaged in a land use survey in 1958. After an introductory chapter, Niddrie covers physical geography, geology, soil erosion, climate, vegetation, fauna, inhabitants (both pre-Columbian and historic), population distribution, language, dialect, and housing. He then traces Tobago's history from the era of colonial rivalries, when the island changed hands many times, down to its present union with Trinidad. The last chapter deals with present-day Tobago: its politics, economy, religion, folk customs, education, planning and development, health and tourism.

4 **Area handbook for Trinidad and Tobago.**
Jan Knippers Black, Howard I. Blutstein, Kathryn Therese Johnston, David S. McMorris. Washington, DC: Government Printing Office, 1976. 304p. map. bibliog.

One of a series of United States government sponsored compilations of information on the social, economic, political, and military aspects of all countries. This teamwork effort, based largely on published sources, should prove useful for its accessible chapters on the nation's geography, demography, history, social systems, living conditions, education, government and politics, economy, and national security. The book includes an unannotated twenty-eight page bibliography.

5 **The Caribbean heritage.**
Virginia Radcliffe. New York: Walker, 1976. 271p. bibliog.

Although this general overview of the Caribbean islands, past and present, contains little which is directly relevant to Trinidad and Tobago, it is an attractive volume whose text and photographs (unfortunately in black and white) succeed nicely in conveying the ambiance of the region.

6 **The aftermath of sovereignty: West Indian perspectives.**
Edited by David Lowenthal, Lambros Comitas. Garden City, New York: Doubleday/Anchor Press, 1973. 422p. bibliog.

This is the final volume in a series of four (preceded by *Slaves, freemen, citizens*; *Work and family life*; and *Consequences of class and color*) in which the editors bring together essays examining the non-Hispanic Caribbean. The majority of the contributions are by West Indians. The book is divided into two sections, each dealing with a major theme of the post-independence era in the region: 'Freedom and power' focuses on politics and government; and 'On being a West Indian' examines national and personal identity after independence. A bibliography of selected readings closes the volume. Essays dealing specifically with Trinidad and Tobago are: Eric Williams's 'Massa day done,' p. 3-29; Gordon K. Lewis's 'The Trinidad and Tobago General Election of 1961,' p. 121-61; K. V. Parmasad's 'By the light of a deya,' p. 283-91; Lloyd Best's 'The February Revolution,' p. 306-29; Desmond Allum's 'Legality vs. morality: a plea for Lt. Raffique Shah,' p. 331-48; V. S. Naipaul's 'Power to the Caribbean people,' p. 363-71; and C. L. R. James's 'The mighty sparrow,' p. 373-81.

7 **The Caribbean islands.**
Mary Slater. New York: Viking Press, 1968. 244p. maps. bibliog. (A Studio Book).

Mary Slater's sharp eye for the physical appearance of the West Indies and her sensitivity to the uniqueness of each island make this volume of particular interest for the architectural information it contains. After a brief general overview of the region, each country receives a separate chapter and Trinidad is covered on p. 214-30.

8 **The small nation with a big contribution.**
Eric Williams. *New Commonwealth, Trade and Commerce*, vol. 45, no. 3 (March 1967), p. 107-09.

Trinidad's then Prime Minister, Dr. Williams, presents the government's aims, policies, and views.

9 **The West Indies chooses a capital.**
David Lowenthal. *Geographical Review*, vol. 48, no. 3 (July 1958), p. 336-64. map.

This article focuses mainly on portraits and self-portraits of three islands – Jamaica, Barbados, and Trinidad – at the time when they were the major contenders for the honour of having the capital of the Federation of the West Indies on their shores. The eight pages on Trinidad paint a realistic – as opposed to a tourist oriented – picture of how the island looks to itself and to its Caribbean neighbours. The reader receives some interesting insights into inter-island rivalries.

Geography

General

10 **Middle America, its lands and peoples.**
Robert C. West, John P. Augelli. Englewood Cliffs, New Jersey: Prentice-Hall, 1976. 2nd ed. 494p. maps. bibliog.

A standard geography with a strong cultural and historical bias. The authors first present five chapters on the culture, physical patterns, geographic parameters, economic geography, population, and political geography of the entire Caribbean-Central American region. Subsequently, each territory receives individual treatment. The islands of Trinidad and Tobago are covered on p. 185-91: their physical and historical setting, economic patterns, industries, agriculture, and population are discussed. Maps of land use are included, and photographs of a Hindu temple and an Episcopal church illustrate the nation's cultural diversity.

11 **The Caribbean islands.**
Helmut Blume, translated from the German by Johannes Maczewski, Ann Norton. London: Longman, 1974. 464p. maps. bibliog.

A thorough survey of the entire Caribbean region. Chapter twenty-three is on Trinidad and Tobago and covers: physical geography, settlement and population, agriculture, mining and industry, transport and trade. Maps show the regional divisions, industry and transport, precipitation and vegetation, and land and farming systems on the island of Trinidad and settlement schemes on Tobago. An excellent sixty-four page bibliography adds to the value of the book, covering geographical literature on the West Indies as a whole and on each territory separately up to 1970.

12 **The West Indies; a geography of the West Indies, with special reference to the Commonwealth islands, and the mainland Commonwealth countries of Guyana and Belize.**
F. C. Evans. London: Cambridge University Press; Trinidad: Columbus Publications, 1973. 128p. maps.

A handy presentation of basic geographical information, for use by the student. After introductory chapters on general topics of physical geography, economic background, and human geography, each island receives an individual treatment: the 'Trinidad and Tobago,' chapter is on p. 43-52. The text is accompanied by maps and aerial photographs.

13 **A first geography of Trinidad & Tobago.**
F. C. Evans. London: Cambridge University Press, 1968. 56p. maps.

An elementary economic geography, intended for use by schoolchildren.

Special aspects

14 **Land use and population in Tobago; an environmental study.**
David L. Niddrie. Bude, Cornwall, England: Geographical Publications, 1961. 59p. map. bibliog. (World Land Use Survey. Regional Monograph, no. 3).

In order to complete this study of Tobagonian land use, Niddrie 'carried out a detailed mapping in the field of the present use and non-use of the land and then, by parallel studies in space and time, has sought to show how the patterns of today are derived from both the present environmental factors and the sequence of historical events in the past.' Sociological and economic, as well as physical, factors are given due weight. The text is accompanied by a map of land use during 1956–58, on a scale of 1 : 63,360, constructed from aerial photographs.

15 **Commercial geography of Trinidad and Tobago.**
Robert C. Kingsbury. Bloomington, Indiana: Department of Geography, Indiana University, 1960. 44p. maps. (Technical Report, no. 4).

A short report on economic conditions and commerce, prepared under contract for the US Office of Naval Research.

16 **Changes in the geography of Trinidad.**
Preston E. James. *Scottish Geographical Magazine*, vol. 73, no. 3 (Dec. 1957), p. 158-66.

A history of land use on the island of Trinidad from the time of its occupation by the British, in 1797, to 1955.

Toponymy

17 **Place names as a reflection of cultural chance: an example from the Lesser Antilles.**

Marjorie Bingham Wesche. *Caribbean Studies*, vol. 12, no. 2 (July 1972), p. 74-98. maps. bibliog.

A study of 'the process by which place names are given, maintained intact, modified, or replaced over a period of time, as related to cultural events and influences throughout that period. . . .' Wesche scrutinizes the place-names of the four so-called 'ceded islands' of the Lesser Antilles: Tobago, Grenada, St. Vincent and Dominica, from 1763 to 1972. Tobago is considered on p. 77-81 and inter-island comparison shows that its place-names have been overwhelmingly English since the establishment of permanent European settlement on the island.

18 **II. Notes of Iere, the Amerindian name for Trinidad.**

K. M. Laurence. *Caribbean Quarterly*, vol. 13, no. 3 (Sept. 1967), p. 45-51. map. bibliog.

Laurence's discussion of the Amerindian name for Trinidad – usually given as a variation of Iere or Caeri – indicates that its meaning is most likely to be simply 'island,' and thus the oft-cited interpretation of the word as 'Land of the Hummingbird,' although picturesque, is inaccurate.

19 **Sur le nom de l'Ile de Tobago.** (On the name of the island of Tobago.)

Jean-Claude Nardin. *Caribbean Studies*, vol. 2, no. 2 (July 1962), p. 31-34.

A well-documented research note on the origin of the name of the island of Tobago, written in French.

Maps and atlases

20 **Atlas of the Caribbean Basin.**

Harry F. Young, edited by Colleen Sussman. *Department of State Bulletin*, vol. 82, no. 2066 (Sept. 1982), not paginated.

A special insert of thirteen unnumbered pages of maps and charts illustrating important strategic and economic features of the Caribbean Basin. The maps and charts are limited to the countries which, like Trinidad and Tobago, are included in the Reagan Administration's Caribbean Basin Initiative. They show political alignments; military balance; membership of international economic organizations; agricultural growth; agricultural exports; manufacturing, refining, and mining exports; export markets; import sources; energy; access to portable water; literacy; and immigration to the United States.

21 **Trinidad and Tobago.**
United States Central Intelligence Agency. Washington, DC: Central Intelligence Agency, 1976. Scale: 1 : 1,000,000.

A coloured map, 22 cm × 17 cm, showing the main towns, roads, and airports on the two islands.

22 **Trinidad.**
Trinidad and Tobago Survey Division. 3rd ed. Port-of-Spain: the author, 1975. Scale: 1 : 150,000.

A detailed coloured map.

23 **Continental shelf boundary: Trinidad & Tobago-Venezuela.**
Office of the Geographer, US Department of State. Washington, DC, 1970. 4p. map. (International Boundary Study, series A; Limits in the Sea, no. 11).

A booklet of text accompanying a map of the continental shelf boundary between Trinidad and Tobago and Venezuela.

Geology

General

24 **Trinidad and Tobago.**
Rhodes W. Fairbridge. In: *The encyclopedia of world regional geology, part 1: Western hemisphere (including Antarctica and Australia*). Edited by Rhodes W. Fairbridge. Stroudsburg, Pennsylvania: Dowden, Hutchinson & Ross, 1975, p. 497-98. bibliog. (Encyclopedia of Earth Sciences, no. 8).

A succinct, authoritative physical description of Trinidad and Tobago.

25 **The overturned anticlime of the Northern Range of Trinidad near Port of Spain.**
Henry C. Potter. *Journal of the Geological Society* (London), vol. 129, pt. 2 (1973), p. 133-38. map. bibliog.

These results of research on the stratigraphy of the Maraval area in Trinidad revise previous geologic conclusions.

26 **Geological map and cross-sections of Trinidad.**
Zurich: O. Fussli; London: E. Stanford, 1959. Scale: 1 : 100,000.

A geological map prepared by H. G. Kugler.

27 **Trinidad.**

H. G. Kugler. In: *Handbook of South American geology; an explanation of the geologic map of South America.* Edited by William F. Jenks, containing papers by A. I. de Oliveira (et al). New York: Geological Society of America, 1956, p. 351-65. map. bibliog. (Geological Society of America, Memoir, no. 65).

A short presentation of the rocks and rock formations of Trinidad, with a stratigraphic table, a geologic map, and a cross-section of the island.

28 **The mud volcanoes of Trinidad.**

K. W. Barr. *Caribbean Quarterly*, vol. 3, no. 2 (Sept. 1953), p. 80-85.

An informative article on a curious natural phenomenon – the mud volcanoes found in southern areas of Trinidad. Trinidad is not a volcanic island and its mud volcanoes are unrelated to the fiery type: their temperatures are not elevated although they exhibit, in miniature, the features of a volcano – erupting intermittently, extruding mud 'lava,' and building up cones. The author explains the physical mechanisms that underlie this process, caused by the seepage of natural hydrocarbon gases from underground. The article also includes a map of the principal sites of mud volcanoes, photographs, and a diagram of a schematic section through a typical mud volcano.

29 **Geology of Tobago, British West Indies.**

John C. Maxwell. *Bulletin of the Geological Society of America*, vol. 59, no. 8 (Aug. 1948), p. 801-54. maps. bibliog.

Based on fieldwork conducted in the summer of 1941 under the auspices of Princeton University, this thorough presentation of Tobagonian geology provides a detailed description of rocks and rock formations on the island. It also includes a summary of the geologic history of Tobago, placing it in the context of the geology of the Eastern Caribbean. The article includes a bibliography of pertinent geologic literature on Tobago to the time of publication. Maps, charts, diagrams, and tables illustrate the text.

30 **Tertiary and Quaternary beds of Tobago, West Indies.**

C. T. Trechmann. *Geological Magazine*, vol. 71, no. 9 (Nov. 1934), p. 481–93. map.

This article on Tertiary and Quaternary rock formations describes and illustrates fossils from the upper Miocene of Tobago. The author also describes the coral rock found in Tobago and contrasts it with that occurring in Barbados.

31 **The geology of Venezuela and Trinidad.**

Ralph Alexander Liddle. Fort Worth, Texas: J. P. MacGowan, 1928. 552p. map. bibliog.

The geology of Trinidad is covered in Part Two, on p. 417-505. Based on fieldwork undertaken from 1920 to 1925, the volume covers physiography, rocks and rock formations, structural geology, and economic geology – asphalt, manjak, and petroleum. The work is enhanced by maps and plates and the bibliography lists the important geologic works dealing with the area.

32 **The geology of the island of Trinidad, B.W.I.**
Gerald A. Waring, with notes on paleontology by G. D. Harris. Baltimore, Maryland: Johns Hopkins Press, 1926. 180p. maps. bibliog. (Johns Hopkins University Studies in Geology, no. 7).

This work is based on data collected during a 1919-1923 survey sponsored by the Trinidad Petroleum Development Company, Ltd. The author states that 'the present paper is intended to bring together the information now available, rather than to be a comprehensive report on the subject.' After a review of previously published materials, cited in bibliographic footnotes, the book covers the stratigraphy, palaeontology, geologic history, and economic geology of the island. Production of petroleum, asphalt, manjak, and other minerals is noted.

33 **Notice of the Pitch Lake of Trinidad.**
N. S. Manross. *American Journal of Science and Arts*, second series, vol. 20, no. 59 (Sept 1855), p. 153-60.

An early, narrative, firsthand description of this remarkable natural phenomenon, a giant reservoir of bitumen, thirty-nine miles south of Port-of-Spain.

Fossils

34 **Fossils from the Northern Range of Trinidad.**
C. T. Trechmann. *Geological Magazine*, vol. 72, no. 850 (April 1935), p. 166–75. map.

Fossils from Laventile, Point Gourde, Gasparee, and Toco are covered. Besides describing these fossils, Trechmann includes a review of the literature pertaining to the Northern Range, and a description of a geological section at Toco Bay.

35 **On some sponges and a coral of Upper Cretaceous Age from Toco Bay, Trinidad.**
H. Dighton Thomas. *Geological Magazine*, vol. 72, no. 850 (April 1935), p. 175-79. bibliog.

Describes the sponges and a coral collected by Dr. C. T. Trechmann at Toco. Specimens are illustrated in plates.

36 **Miocene gastropods and scaphopods from Trinidad, British West Indies.**
Wendell C. Mansfield. *U.S. National Museum. Proceedings*, vol. 66, no. 2559 (1925) p. 1-65.

Describes fossil shells from a few locations in Trinidad and determines, 'in so far as is practicable, their stratigraphic position with respect to the standard section of the Atlantic and Gulf Coastal Plain and the West Indies.' Illustrated with plates.

37 **A Pleistocene flora from the island of Trinidad.**
Edward W. Berry. *U.S. National Museum. Proceedings*, vol. 66, no. 2558 (1925), p. 1-9.

A description of fossil leaves from strata near the village of Oropouche with four pages of plates.

38 **The Tertiary flora of the island of Trinidad, B.W.I.**
Edward W. Berry. In: *Contributions to the geology and paleontology of South America; five papers*. Edward W. Berry, Frank M. Swartz. Baltimore, Maryland: Johns Hopkins Press, 1925, p. 71-181. (Johns Hopkins University Studies in Geology, no. 6).

In this study of fossil plants found in the Tertiary of Trinidad, Berry covers fifty-one species collected mainly by H. G. Kugler and which are now in the collection of Johns Hopkins University.

39 **Descriptions of Tertiary fossils from the Antillean region.**
R. J. Lechmere Guppy, William Healey Dall. *U.S. National Museum. Proceedings*, vol. 19, no. 1110 (1897), p. 303-31.

Guppy contributes descriptions of fifteen new species of fossil molluscs from Trinidad.

Travel Guides

40 **Fielding's economy Caribbean 1986.**
Margaret Zellers. New York: William Morrow, 1986. 272p.

Thrift is the keynote of this annually updated tourist guide to the Caribbean islands. The volume includes and evaluates more than 400 low-budget accommodations: small hotels, inns, guesthouses, apartments, cottages, and campsites.

41 **Fielding's Caribbean 1986.**
Margaret Zellers. New York: William Morrow, 1986. 784p. maps.

An annually updated work by one of America's major producers of guidebooks. It utilizes a star system to rate accommodations and provides standard tourist information for the islands.

42 **Fodor's Caribbean and the Bahamas 1985.**
New York: Fodor's Travel Guides, 1985. 670p. maps.

Contains historical, political, and social background as well as predictable guidebook information for the area. Colour photographs impart the atmosphere of the region, and the volume includes maps and city plans.

43 **Fodor's budget Caribbean.**
New York: Fodor's Travel Guides, 1985. 304p.

Provides tourist information with an emphasis on cost cutting.

44 **The 1985 South American handbook.**
Edited by John Brooks, associate editors Joyce Candy, Ben Box. Bath, England: Trade & Travel Publications, 1984. 61st annual ed. 1,438p. maps.

The 'Trinidad and Tobago' chapter is on p. 1,343-351. It provides compact, although detailed information on the country, covering both background – history, government, politics, economy – and tourist needs – hotels, restaurants, entertainment, rentals, documents, tipping, holidays, climate, clothing, etc.

45 **A cruising guide to the Caribbean and the Bahamas; including the north coast of South America, Central America, and Yucatan.**
Jerrems C. Hart, William T. Stone, Jolyon Byerley. New York: Dodd Mead, 1982. rev. ed. 626p. maps. bibliog. (Triton Boating Book).

This cruising handbook provides the sailor with the necessary maps, charts, diagrams, and other information needed for yachting on the Caribbean Sea.

46 **The pocket guide to the West Indies and British Guiana, British Honduras, Bermuda, the Spanish Main, Surinam & the Panama Canal.**
Sir Algernon Aspinall, revised by J. Sydney Dash. London: Methuen, 1954. 10th ed. Reprinted with corrections, London: Methuen, 1960. 474p. maps. bibliog.

Aspinall's guidebook was first published in 1907, and has been through many editions. Although now obviously outdated in many respects, this is one of the travel guides that remain a goldmine of miscellaneous geographical, historical, and architectural information. It also is of some historical interest in itself for the portrait it presents of Trinidad in Crown Colony days. Now out of print, anyone who has a copy would be well-advised not to discard it.

Travellers' Accounts

47 **Travel accounts and descriptions of Latin America and the Caribbean, 1800-1920; a selected bibliography.**
Compiled by Thomas L. Welch, Myriam Figueras, with a foreword by Val. T. McComie. Washington, DC: Columbus Memorial Library, Organization of American States, 1982. 293p.

The Trinidad and Tobago section is on p. 242–46 and consists of an unannotated list of books by twenty-one authors. The criterion for inclusion in the bibliography is that 'a work [has] to be by a writer who was not a native of the area and who recorded his impressions and observations between 1800 and 1920.' The titles can all be found in the Columbus Memorial Library in Washington, DC.

48 **Trinidad and Tobago: isles of the immortelles.**
Robin Bryans. London: Faber, 1967. 306p. maps.

Bryans, who visited Trinidad and Tobago in the mid-1960s, intersperses this first-person account of his experiences in the newly-independent nation with history and legends from its colonial past.

49 **Letter from Port of Spain.**
Bernard Taper. *New Yorker* (23 Oct. 1965), p. 203-26.

A smoothly written essay in which Taper recounts his 1965 visit to Port-of-Spain, during which he attended the Steel Band Music Festival and interviewed Prime Minister Eric Williams. Taper also gives his speculations on the reasons behind the disintegration of the West Indian Federation.

50 **Revolt in the tropics; travels in the Caribbean.**
Karl Eskelund. London: Alvin Redman, 1963. 176p. map.

Veteran Danish traveller Karl Eskelund and his Chinese-born wife Chi-yun travelled through the Caribbean from Cuba to British Guiana in the early 1960s.

His personal impressions of Trinidad are presented in three chapters of this book: 'Potpourri,' focuses on the racial composition of Trinidadian society; 'The Holy Man' recounts a visit to an East Indian sage; and 'Christmas in Shanty Town' describes a holiday celebration in a poor Black section of Port-of-Spain.

51 **The middle passage; impressions of five societies – British, French and Dutch – in the West Indies and South America.**
V. S. Naipaul. London: Andre Deutsch, 1962. 232p.

Chapter two of this book focuses on the novelist Naipaul's account of his return visit to his native Trinidad in 1960, and amounts to an indictment of the nation and its citizens. Naipaul sounds his theme of Trinidad as an uncreative society in which mimicry and fraudulence predominate. With this said, it should be added that for all its largely unfavourable picture of Trinidad, coloured by Naipaul's deep-seated hostility to the island and its people, the work is well-written and, whether or not one agrees with him, there is much food for thought in Naipaul's observations. The book takes its epigraph from James Anthony Froude's *English in the West Indies* (1887), and has proved to be as controversial as the earlier tome.

52 **Happy-go-lucky Trinidad and Tobago.**
Charles Allmon. *National Geographic Magazine*, vol. 103, no. 1 (Jan. 1953), p. 35-75. maps.

Allmon spent three months touring the two islands during the last decade of British colonialism, and his on-the-spot-reportage nicely captures the feeling of the multi-cultural society. Although emphasis is on the picturesque, Allmon does include facts about such varied topics as religion, music, natural phenomena (including an interesting account of his visit to the Pitch Lake), industry, and agriculture. The article is illustrated with photographs, including a full-page photograph of Red House.

53 **The traveller's tree; a journey through the Caribbean islands.**
Patrick Leigh Fermor, with illustrations by A. Costa. New York: Harper; London: Murray, 1950. 403p. map.

An indefatigable traveller, Fermor responded to Trinidad's exuberance and brio. This book has recently (1984) been reissued in paperback by Penguin Books in its Travellers Library series.

54 **West Indian summer: a retrospect.**
James Pope-Hennessy. London: Batsford, 1943. 117p. map.

In 1939, Pope-Hennessy spent six months as personal secretary to the Governor of Trinidad, Sir Hubert Young. During this time he found both the tropics and colonial high society uncongenial to say the least. Back in London he wrote this book, in which he links the experiences of nine other English travellers to the West Indies (Sir Walter Ralegh, Anthony Trollope, James Anthony Froude, John A. Waller, Henry Nelson Coleridge, A. C. Carmichael, Sir Hans Sloane, Charles Kingsley, and Sir Robert Dudley) with his own impressions.

55 **Glory dead.**
Arthur Calder-Marshall. London: Joseph, 1939. 286p.

Calder-Marshall, a prolific professional writer who distinguished himself in many genres, visited Trinidad in 1938. This book describes the society, customs, and folklore of the island that he observed during his sojourn in Port-of-Spain.

56 **Caribbee cruise; a book of the West Indies.**
John W. Vandercook. New York: Reynal & Hitchcock, 1938. 349p.

Includes an interesting description, on p. 256-76, of Trinidad in 1938 by the author of the detective novel *Murder in Trinidad* (q.v.). Vandercook includes references to the island's folklore.

57 **Sky roaming above two continents; an aerial cruise, with many landings in the countries and islands that circle the Caribbean.**
Harry A. Franck. New York: Frederick A. Stokes Company, 1938. 362p. map.

The American author of many travel books, Franck modernized the Caribbean cruise by substituting the aeroplane for the boat. Chapter XIV of this book recounts his impressions of Trinidad. Franck has a sharp eye for detail and has done his homework on the island. His first-hand impressions, set against the island's history and folklore, still make entertaining reading.

58 **If crab no walk; a traveller in the West Indies.**
Owen Rutter. London: Hutchinson, 1933. 288p. bibliog.

The personal impressions and observations of an Englishman – a professional writer and sophisticated traveller – who had access to Trinidad's top society when he visited the British Caribbean in 1933. In the five chapters of this book devoted to Trinidad, Rutter's comments are self-assured and somewhat complacently racist, but always lively. One chapter includes an account of his meeting with Captain Arthur Cipriani.

59 **Combing the Caribbees.**
Harry L. Foster. New York: Dodd, Mead & Company, 1929. 302p. map.

An American sailing among the islands, Foster offers superficial observations on Trinidad, combining praise for the British Empire with crude racist remarks.

60 **The cradle of the deep; an account of a voyage to the West Indies.**
Sir Frederick Treves. New York: Dutton, 1920. 378p. maps.

Sir Frederick seems to have left no island in the West Indies unvisited. This volume includes a lengthy description of Trinidad as he found it in 1908, as well as stories from the island's history and legends. Interesting photographs accompany the text.

61 **At last, a Christmas in the West Indies.**
Charles Kingsley. London, New York: Macmillan, 1903. 418p. (Life and Works of Charles Kingsley in Nineteen Volumes, vol. 17).

In December, 1869, Kingsley sailed to the West Indies aboard the steamer *Shannon*, reaching Trinidad on 21 December. He spent seven weeks on the island and in this book recounts his travels and experiences in the colony. He visited Port-of-Spain, stayed in a West Indian countryhouse, sailed to the islands of the Bocas, and travelled to the High Woods, the Pitch Lake, San Josef, the Naparima and Montserrat districts, and the Northern mountains. His observations include much natural description, at which he excels; he is sensitive to and appreciates the lush beauty of the islands, although he shows little sympathy for the non-English aspects of colonial life. This book was first published in 1871.

62 **The English in the West Indies; or, the bow of Ulysses.**
James Anthony Froude, with illustrations engraved on wood by G. Pearson, after drawings by the author. New York: Scribner's, 1888. Reprinted, New York: Negro Universities Press, 1969. 373p.

The British historian's visit to the West Indies in 1887 resulted in this classic of racist ideology. Froude devotes two chapters to Trinidad, where he called on Governor Sir William Robinson, was impressed with the island's tropically exuberant nature, and saw everywhere 'the boundless happiness of the black race.' His emphasis is on the folly of granting any sort of political power or home rule to the island's inhabitants, because it would mean rule by Blacks, which to Froude is unthinkable on the grounds of insurmountable racial inferiority. The Trinidadian scholar J. J. Thomas provides a critique of Froude's views in his *Froudacity; West Indian fables by James Anthony Froude explained* (London: T. Fisher Unwin, 1889), which has been reprinted with an introduction by C. L. R. James and a biographical note by Donald Wood (London: New Beacon, 1969).

63 **The ordeal of free labor in the British West Indies.**
William G. Sewell. London: Sampson, Low, 1862. 2nd ed., new impression. Reprinted, London: Cass, 1968. 325p. (Cass Library of West Indian Studies, no. 3).

Sewell visited the British West Indies in 1859 in order to report to American readers on the results of twenty years of Black emancipation. This work originally appeared in the *New York Times*. A large section is devoted to Trinidad (p. 95-140), characterizing the island in the mid-19th century. Sewell describes the Creoles of African descent, the new immigrants from Asia, and the agriculture and commerce of the country. He took a favourable view of emancipation, feeling it had contributed to the prosperity of the British West Indies. He also found the indenture system well-regulated. Another first hand description of Trinidad in the mid-19th century can be found in Charles William Day's *Five years' residence in the West Indies* (London: Coburn & Company, 1852).

Travellers' Accounts

64 **The West Indies: their social and religious condition.**
Edward Bean Underhill. London: Jackson, Walford & Hadden, 1862. Reprinted, Westport, Connecticut: Negro Universities Press, 1970. 493p.

This work is the result of a tour undertaken in 1860 'to investigate the religious condition of the numerous Baptist Churches' in the West Indies. Underhill views the island inhabitants from a sympathetic perspective – a rare viewpoint among British travellers of the time. In his three chapters on Trinidad he describes Port-of-Spain and San Fernando and discusses East Indian immigration to the country.

65 **The West Indies and the Spanish Main.**
Anthony Trollope. London: Chapman & Hall, 1860. Reprinted, London: Cass, 1968. 395p. map. (Cass Library Of West Indian Studies, no. 2).

The Victorian novelist Trollope's account of his sojourn in the West Indies in 1859. Chapter fourteen describes his visit to Trinidad, which he found picturesque. Although he spent only two days on the island, he manages to produce seventeen pages of description and comment.

66 **Six months in the West Indies in 1825.**
[Henry Nelson Coleridge]. London: John Murray, 1825. Reprinted, New York: Negro Universities Press, 1970. 332p.

Henry Nelson Coleridge accompanied his uncle, William H. Coleridge, the first Bishop of Barbados, through the West Indies in 1825. His visit to Trinidad, where he was entertained by Sir Ralph Woodford, is described on pages [63]-103 of his book. His observations on the island and its population of planters and slaves are sunny and superficial.

67 **A tour through the several islands of Barbados, St. Vincent, Antigua, Tobago, and Grenada, in the years 1791 and 1792.**
William Young. In: *The history, civil and commercial of the British West Indies. With a continuation to the present time.* Bryan Edwards. London: G. and W. B. Whittaker, 1818-1819. 5th ed. vol. 3, p. 243-84. maps. Reprinted, New York: AMS Press, 1966. 5 vols.

Young was a West Indian proprietor who visited his estate on Tobago in 1791. His account of this visit contains some interesting observations on the social mores of the time. Young was appointed governor of the island in 1807, an office he filled until his death in 1815. A map of Tobago in the 1790s supplements the text.

Flora and Fauna

General

68 **A naturalist in Trinidad.**
C. Brooke Worth, drawings by Don R. Eckelberry. Philadelphia: Lippincott, 1967. 291p. map.

From 1960 to 1965 Worth was attached to the Trinidad Regional Virus Laboratory. This first-person account of his adventures while stationed there contains informative chapters on Trinidad's fauna: monkeys, small mammals, spiders and bugs, vultures, bees, snails, ants, birds, bats, snakes, lizards and caymans, swifts, and hummingbirds and butterflies.

69 **Caribbean treasure.**
Ivan T. Sanderson. London: Hamish Hamilton, 1940; New York: Viking Press, 1939. 292p. map.

Sanderson, a British zoologist, includes an account of his specimen-collecting in Trinidad.

Plants

70 **Some folk medicinal plants from Trinidad.**
Wesley Wong. *Economic Botany*, vol. 30, no. 2 (April-June 1976), p. 103-42. bibliog.

Based on data gathered in 1966 and 1967 in the village of Blanchisseuse, the major part of this article consists of a taxonomic table of 186 Trinidadian plants to which therapeutic properties have been ascribed. For each plant, the taxonomic name, common name, medicinal use, and biodynamics are furnished.

71 **The useful and ornamental plants in Trinidad and Tobago.**
R. O. Williams, R. O. Williams, Jr. Port-of-Spain: Guardian Commercial Printery, 1951. 4th rev. ed. 335p. bibliog.

This volume, the most recent revision of a standard work, provides a complete list of the plant resources of the islands. The original edition was prepared in 1927 by W. G. Freeman and R. O. Williams.

72 **The natural vegetation of the island of Tobago, British West Indies.**
J. S. Beard. *Ecological Monographs*, vol. 14, no. 2 (April 1944), p. 135-63. maps. bibliog.

The author, who was Assistant Conservator of Forests in the Colonial Forest Service, notes that although the flora of Tobago has been exhaustively described, little attention has been paid to its ecology. His article is intended to remedy this situation. Beard's ecological description is confined to 'those areas of virgin forest, woodland, and swamp which have not yet been destroyed or radically altered by human interference.' Covering environmental factors, flora, and plant communities, this thorough presentation of the ecology of the island in 1944 is enhanced with tables, diagrams, photographs, and maps. Beard is also the author of a book dealing in a similar way with the ecology and flora of Trinidad: *The natural vegetation of Trinidad* (Oxford: Clarenden Press, 1946).

73 **Some impressions of the flora of Guiana and Trinidad.**
Douglass Houghton Campbell. *Popular Science Monthly*, vol. 82, [no issue no.] (Jan. 1913), p. 19-32.

In this rambling account of a visit to Surinam and Trinidad, Campbell comments on the island's botanical abundance.

Bats

74 **Trinidad and bat research.**
Arthur M. Greenhall. *Natural History*, vol. 74, no. 6 (June-July 1965), p. 14-21.

Trinidad is in the forefront in the study of bat ecology, the epidemiology of bat-associated diseases, and methods of bat control. In this popular article, Arthur M. Greenhall discusses Trinidad's varied bat fauna with both knowledge and style. The reader will be fascinated by his presentation of the bats of the island, which include *Vampyrum spectrum* ('the largest New World bat, with a three-foot wingspan and a rat-sized body'), the rare white-winged vampire *Diaemus youngi*, and the weirdly wrinkle-faced *Centurio senex*. Illustrated with photographs.

75 **A review of the bats of Trinidad and Tobago.**
George O. Goodwin, A. M. Greenhall. *American Museum of Natural History Bulletin*, vol. 122, art. 3 (1961), p. 187-302.

A comprehensive treatise on the bat population of the two islands. Dr. Greenhall has also contributed a brief 'Check list of the bats of Trinidad and Tobago' to the *Caribbean Medical Journal* (vol. 21, nos. 1–4, 1959).

76 **Portrait of a vampire.**
Joseph Bernstein. *Natural History*, vol. 61, no. 2 (Feb. 1952), p. 82-87 and ff.

A popular account of outbreaks of rabies among both animals and humans in 20th-century Trinidad in which the rabies virus was found to have been transmitted by the bite of the vampire bat. Bernstein describes this bat's habits and the measures taken against the 1950 outbreak. Illustrated with photographs.

Birds

77 **A guide to the birds of Trinidad and Tobago.**
Richard Ffrench, illustrations by John P. O'Neill. Valley Forge, Pennsylvania: Harrowood Books, 1976. rev. ed. 470p. bibliog. (Publication of the Asa Wright Nature Center, no. 1).

This book, which was sponsored by the Cornell University Laboratory of Ornithology, lists and describes 350 avian species. Richard Ffrench has not only written of the avian species of Trinidad and Tobago, but has also led bird-watching tours of the islands.

78 **Courtship behavior of the Greater Bird of Paradise.**
James J. Dinsmore. *The Auk*, vol. 87, no. 2 (April 1970), p. 305-21. bibliog.

During 1965-1966, Dinsmore conducted zoological fieldwork on Little Tobago and located seven birds of paradise. He observed 304 courtship displays and heard an additional 168. This article describes and discusses the display grounds, the calls, the courtship display, and the seasonal activities of birds of paradise and provides a bibliography of literature on the species.

79 **Dual calling by birds of paradise.**
James J. Dinsmore. *The Auk*, vol. 86, no. 1 (Jan. 1969), p. 139-40.

Dinsmore describes the call of the *Paradisaea apoda* of Little Tobago as he heard it in 1965-66.

80 **The birds of Trinidad and Tobago.**
G. A. C. Herklots. London: Collins, 1961. 287p. map. bibliog.

This volume is illustrated with sixteen colour plates by the author, four black and white plates by J. M. Abbott, and fourteen text figures.

81 **Feathered dancers of Little Tobago.**
E. Thomas Gilliard. *National Geographic Magazine*, vol. 114, no. 3 (Sept. 1958), p. 428-40. map.

A popular account of an expedition led by Gilliard, who was Associate Curator of Birds at the American Museum of Natural History, to discover whether the courtship dance of the Greater Bird of Paradise was fact or fiction – and, if fact, to capture it on film. Gilliard found that the gaudily-plumed species did indeed perform the ritual as reported. The article includes the first colour pictures of the golden-feathered birds in the courtship display, photographed by Frederick Kent Truslow.

82 **Strange courtship of birds of paradise.**
Dillon Ripley. *National Geographic Magazine*, vol. 97, no. 2 (Feb. 1950), p. 247-78.

Although this article by ornithologist Ripley deals with the species in New Guinea, it includes a description of the courtship dance of *Paradisaea apoda*, the Greater Bird of Paradise that was introduced into Little Tobago. The description, as given by Alfred Russel Wallace appears on page 268 of this article. Ripley comments that '[Wallace's] description of the courting birds, first published in 1869, is as good today as it was then.' Illustrations of the Greater Bird of Paradise are among those accompanying the article.

Shells

83 **Sea shells of the West Indies: a guide to the marine molluscs of the Caribbean.**
Michael Humfrey. London: Collins; New York: Taplinger, 1975. 351p. maps. bibliog.

The author, an amateur conchologist of high repute, describes 497 shells of the Caribbean. The volume contains coloured illustrations.

84 **A field guide to shells of the Atlantic and Gulf coasts and the West Indies.**
Percy A. Morris, edited by William J. Clench. Boston, Massachusetts: Houghton Mifflin, 1973. 3rd ed. 330p. bibliog. (Peterson Field Guide Series).

Describes 1,035 species of Caribbean shells, all but two of which are illustrated by one or more photographs. English common names as well as Latin scientific names are given.

85 **Notes on the land-shells of Trinidad, Grenada and Dominica, and also of Curacao and Buen Ayre, W.I.**
Thomas Bland. *American Journal of Conchology*, new series, vol. 4, no. 4 (1868), p. 177-92.

Bland is the author of the 'Catalogue of land-shells of the West Indies,' in the *Annals of the Lyceum*, vol. 7, (1861). These notes supplement the earlier work. The section on Trinidad (p. 178-87), lists and describes thirty-eight species of land-shells.

Prehistory and Archaeology

Pre-Columbian inhabitants

86 **Aboriginal Trinidad in the 16th century.**
Stephen D. Glazier. *Florida Anthropologist*, vol. 33, no. 3 (Sept. 1980), p. 152-59.

Glazier puts forth the view that Carib-speaking tribes shared protohistoric Trinidad with the Arawak.

87 **A revised aboriginal ethnohistory of Trinidad.**
Alfredo E. Figuerdo, Stephen D. Glazier. In: *Proceedings of the International Congress for the study of Pre-Columbian cultures of the Lesser Antilles, VII, Montreal, Canada, 1978*. Montreal: Université de Montréal, Centre de Recherches Caraïbes, 1978, p. 259-62. bibliog.

Evidence points to there having been Carib-speaking Indians as well as Arawakan tribes in 16th-century Trinidad. Aboriginal culture appears to have been more closely related to mainland Tropical Forest groups than to that of Circum-Caribbean tribes.

88 **Trade and warfare in protohistoric Trinidad.**
Stephen D. Glazier. In: *Proceedings of the International Congress for the study of Pre-Columbian cultures of the Lesser Antilles, VII, Montreal, Canada, 1978*. Montreal: Université de Montréal, Centre de Recherches Caraïbes, 1978, p. 279-82. bibliog.

Studies trade and warfare among 16th-century Trindad's aboriginal population.

89 **Prehistory of the West Indies.**
Irving Rouse. *Science*, vol. 144, no. 3618 (May 1, 1964), p. 499-513. maps.

Although this article does not deal directly with Trinidad, it is a readable, authoritative presentation of conclusions drawn from research as to whence, when, and how the Indians of the Caribbean region came to be where Columbus encountered them.

90 **The aborigines of Trinidad.**
J. A. Bullbrook. Port-of-Spain: Royal Victoria Institute Museum, 1960. 60p. (Occasional Papers, no. 2).

A summary of the history of Trinidad's archaeology that discusses aboriginal sites and artifacts and presents a good picture of the island's pre-Columbian inhabitants.

91 **The aboriginal remains of Trinidad and the West Indies.**
J. A. Bullbrook. *Caribbean Quarterly*, vol. 1, no. 1 (April-May-June 1949), p. 16-21.

This is the first of a two-part series of articles in which Bullbrook summarizes what is known about the Arawak, the stone age Indian tribe inhabiting the island of Trinidad when it was discovered by Columbus. In this first segment, Bullbrook describes the Arawaks' living conditions and food.

92 **The aboriginal remains of Trinidad and the West Indies – II.**
J. A. Bullbrook. *Caribbean Quarterly*, vol. 1, no. 2 (July-August-Sept. 1949), p. 10-15.

Bullbrook continues the story of the Trinidad Arawak, describing their tools and weapons, dress and personal ornaments, religious beliefs, and origins and contacts.

93 **Origin of the Tainan culture, West Indies.**
Sven Loven. Gothenburg, Sweden: Elanders, 1935. 696p. map. Reprinted, New York: AMS Press, 1979.

This revised second edition of Loven's *Über die Wurzeln der tainischen Kultur* is a fundamental treatise on the Taino culture of the West Indies. The book summarizes what was known of Trinidad's Amerindians to 1935.

Aboriginal sites and artifacts

94 **On the excavation of a shell mound at Palo Seco, Trinidad, B.W.I.**
J. A. Bullbrook, edited and with an appendix by Irving Rouse. New Haven, Connecticut: Yale University Press for the Department of Anthropology, Yale University, 1953. 114p. maps. bibliog. (Yale University Publications in Anthropology, no. 50).

This important monograph, written in 1919, although not published until 1953, concerns the Palo Seco midden as Bullbrook excavated it in that year. It is a pioneer treatise in its detailed stratigraphic analysis, the first in the Antilles, and in its thorough reconstruction of Palo Seco culture. In a preface, Bullbrook traces the history of archaeology in Trinidad from 1898. The text is a meticulously detailed description of the archaeological findings at the excavation: pottery, stone artifacts, bone artifacts, shells, animal remains, and human remains. Bullbrook builds up the history of the people of Palo Seco from his findings, and also compares the Palo Seco antiquities with those from the Erin midden, the Mayaro midden, and with antiquities from other islands of the Antilles and from the South American continent. In an appendix to the volume, 'Indian sites in Trinidad,' Irving Rouse discusses cultures and styles. The volume includes a map of Indian sites and a lengthy bibliography.

95 **Notes on a find from Trinidad.**
Frederick W. Sleight. *American Antiquity*, vol. 11, no. 4 (April 1946), p. 260-61.

A brief report of a prehistoric pottery vessel found in Trinidad, along with a photograph of the object.

96 **Certain archaeological investigations in Trinidad, British West Indies.**
Theodoor de Booy. *American Anthropologist*, new series, vol. 19, no. 4 (Oct.-Dec. 1917), p. 471-86.

De Booy records excavations made in shell-heaps on the St. Bernard estate near Cape Mayaro during the summer of 1915, where he found pottery vessels, bowls, and other objects. Selected artifacts are illustrated in plates.

97 **Prehistoric objects from a shell-heap at Erin Bay, Trinidad.**
J. Walter Fewkes. *American Anthropologist*, vol. 16, no. 2 (April-June 1914), p. 200-20.

Fewkes made excavations in a shell-heap at Erin Bay in 1912-1913. In this article he describes the pottery, stone, bone, and wood objects uncovered, and compares prehistoric objects from Trinidad with those found in other Caribbean islands. Plates show the pottery objects.

98 **Prehistoric antiquities from the Antilles in the British Museum.**
T. A. Joyce. *Journal of the Royal Anthropological Institute of Great Britain and Ireland*, vol. 37 (July-Dec. 1907), p. 402-19.

Detailed descriptions, well-illustrated with plates and line drawings, of the most important objects from the West Indies in the British national collection. Only a few of the prehistoric artifacts can definitely be identified as originating in Trinidad.

Environment and Conservation

99 **The natural resources of Trinidad and Tobago.**
Edited by St. G. C. Cooper, P. R. Bacon. London: Edward Arnold, 1981. 223p. maps. bibliog.

Contains essays by various authors on Trinidad and Tobago's environment and its present and projected role in the nation's economy. Part one covers Trinidad and Tobago's physical resources – climate, geology, soil, minerals, water, and energy; part two deals with biological resources – phytochemicals, aquatic resources, forests and agriculture; and part three discusses human resources. This is a readable volume, aimed at the general reader, with bibliographies following each essay, and useful appendixes listing plants, animals, and fruits of economic importance.

100 **Roosting birds and the danger of a gas barge.**
Timothy Green. *Smithsonian*, vol. 6, no. 2 (May 1975), p. 34-41.

Describes Trinidad's first serious conservation battle, which took place in the Caroni Swamp when a gas barge of the Trinidad and Tobago Oil Company was scheduled to run through the sanctuary of the scarlet ibis, Trinidad's national bird. Impressive full-colour photographs of the spectacular bird complement the text.

101 **Conservation and Caribbean regional progress.**
Carl A. Carlozzi, Alice A. Carlozzi. N.p.: Antioch Press for the Caribbean Research Institute, St. Thomas, U.S.V.I., 1968. 151p.

A three-part study of the Eastern Caribbean covering background conditions, resources, and conservation possibilities. Part two is 'an island-by-island inventory of places which have potential for development as national parks, nature reserves, historical sites, or public outdoor recreation areas.' The islands of Tobago and Trinidad are discussed on p. 74-83.

Historiography

102 **British historians and the West Indies.**
Eric Williams, preface by Alan Bullock. New York: Africana Publishing Corporation, 1966. 238p. bibliog.

Williams utilizes a West Indian perspective in this important analysis of British historical scholarship concerned with the Caribbean area. Of the historians who wrote of Trinidad, Froude, Trollope, and Reginald Coupland are criticized in this volume.

103 **Colonialism in Trinidad and Tobago.**
K. O. Laurence. *Caribbean Quarterly*, vol. 9, no. 3 (Sept. 1963). p. 44-56.

A critical and comparative review of Eric Williams's *History of the people of Trinidad and Tobago* and Gertrude Carmichael's *History of the West Indian islands of Trinidad and Tobago*.

104 **A study of the historigraphy of the British West Indies, to the end of the nineteenth century.**
Elsa V. Goveia. Mexico City: Pan American Institute of Geography and History, 1956. (Pan American Institute of Geography & History, Publicacion no. 186; Historigrafias, no. 2; Pan American Institute of Geography & History, Comision de Historia, Publicacion no. 78). Reprinted, Washington, DC: Howard University Press, 1980. 192p. bibliog.

A first-rate critique of historical writings on the British West Indies that were composed between the 17th and the 19th centuries. Goveia points out the assumptions made by the various authors who attempted to record the history of the area and what these assumptions imply. The book covers both general histories of the region and five works: E. L. Joseph's *History of Trinidad* (q.v.), W. H. Gamble's *Trinidad: historical and descriptive . . .* (q.v.), H. I. Woodcock's *A history of Trinidad* (q.v.), Pierre-Gustave-Louis Borde's *Histoire de l'Ille de Trinidad sous le gouvernement espagnole* (q.v.), and L. M. Fraser's *History of Trinidad* (q.v.) that deal particularly with Trinidad and/or Tobago.

History

General

105 **Profile Trinidad; an historical survey from the discovery to 1900.**
Michael Anthony. London: Macmillan Caribbean, 1975. 198p. maps.

This introductory account, which is suitable for undergraduate students or the general reader, of Trinidad's history from 1498 to the beginning of the 20th century focuses particularly on the historical personalities who were at the centre of events, but also includes chapters on the 19th-century immigration to Trinidad by Portuguese, West Indians, Americans, Africans, Europeans, East Indians, and Chinese. Appendix A lists the governors of Trinidad; Spanish from 1506 to 1797 and British from 1797 to 1900. Appendix B is a list of Port-of-Spain street names. The volume is pleasantly illustrated with drawings, maps, and photographs.

106 **History of the people of Trinidad and Tobago.**
Eric Williams. Port-of-Spain: PNM; New York: Praeger, 1962. 204p. maps. bibliog.

A comprehensive scholarly history of Trinidad and Tobago by the nation's first prime minister. Williams wrote this book in a single month in order to have it ready for Trinidad and Tobago's Independence Day, 31 August 1962.

107 **A history of Tobago.**
Henry Iles Woodcock. Ayrshire, Scotland: Smith & Grant, 1867. Reprinted, London: Cass, 1971. 210p. (Cass Library of West Indian Studies, no. 28).

This book, by a former Chief Justice of Tobago, is based on published sources and covers the history of the island from its discovery to 1860. An interesting incidental fact is that Tobago was once the residence of John Paul Jones.

108 **History of the West Indian islands of Trinidad and Tobago, 1498-1900.**
Gertrude Carmichael. London: A. Redman, 1961. 463p. bibliog.

Carmichael was the first to attempt a modern scholarly history of Trinidad and Tobago. The volume emphasizes facts rather than interpretation.

109 **La mise en valeur de l'île de Tabago 1763-1783.** (The development of the island of Tobago 1763-1783.)
Jean Claude Nardin. Paris, The Hague: Mouton, 1969. 357p. maps. bibliog. (Le Monde d'Outre-mer, Passé et Présent. 1. sér. Etude, 31).

A general history of the development of Tobago from 1763 to 1783, which includes a lengthy bibliography.

110 **A history of modern Trinidad, 1783-1962.**
Bridget Brereton. Kingston, Port-of-Spain, London: Heinemann, 1981. 262p. maps. bibliog.

A handy summary of the history of Trinidad as a British colony. Brereton states that her 'major purpose . . . is to synthesize and interpret for a wider public the recent work by researchers and academicians.' Tobago's history is included after 1889, when that island was linked administratively to Trinidad. Attention is paid to economic and social as well as political trends. The volume includes a 'Chronology of major events, 1498-1962' and a short bibliography.

111 **The Legislative Council of Trinidad and Tobago.**
Hewan Craig. London: Faber & Faber, 1952. 195p. map. bibliog.

A straightforward history of the Legislative Council from 1831 to 1950, concentrating on the period 1925 to 1940.

112 **Sources of West Indian history.**
F. R. Augier, Shirley C. Gordon. London: Longmans, 1962. 308p.

A book 'primarily intended for use in the senior forms of secondary schools. It is not a history in itself but a collection of [extracts taken from] various accounts written about many of the events which have taken place in the West Indies.' The selections are grouped topically: people of the Caribbean, economic life, government and politics, religion and education before emancipation, slavery and its abolition, emancipation and apprenticeship, social conditions since emancipation, and attempts at unification from 1831 to 1958. A valuable selection of documents pertaining to Trinidad and Tobago are included in the volume.

Spanish colonial period, 1498-1797

113 **Aboriginal and Spanish colonial Trinidad; a study in culture contact.**
Linda A. Newson. London, New York: Academic Press, 1976. 344p. maps. bibliog.

This valuable book on a neglected topic will provide its reader with a goldmine of information on the archaeological, ecological, and political aspects of Trinidad in both its pre-Columbian and Spanish colonial periods. Newson states in the preface that her book 'is an attempt to analyse the cultural changes that occurred in Trinidad as a result of the discovery and occupation of the island by the Spanish.' She looks at overall changes in the nature of Indian groups and the impact of different Spanish institutions on the Indian culture, covering both the pre-Spanish ecology, population, and economy of the aboriginal inhabitants and the changes that took place on the island during three centuries of Spanish rule: the discovery and conquest (1498-1592); colonization (1592-1776); and colonial reorganization (1776-1797). The volume is exhaustively documented.

114 **Trinidad, provincia de Venezuela; historia de la administracion española de Trinidad.** (Trinidad, province of Venezuela; history of the Spanish administration of Trinidad.)
Jesse A. Noel. Caracas: Academia Nacional de la Historia, 1972. 270p. maps. bibliog. (Fuentes Para la Historia Colonial de Venezuela; Biblioteca de la Academia Nacional de la Historia, no. 109).

A history of the administration of Trinidad during the period when the island formed part of Spain's colonial empire. Noel emphasizes the years 1777 to 1797, when the Spanish undertook an initiative to revitalize the island's economy. Includes a chapter on the British seizure of the island in 1797.

115 **The loss of El Dorado; a history.**
V. S. Naipaul. New York: Penguin Books, 1973. 394p. bibliog. maps.

The well-known novelist centres his book on two striking episodes in Trinidad's history: Sir Walter Ralegh's quest for 'El Dorado,' the Indians' fabled land of gold lying somewhere on the South American mainland, and the trial of Thomas Picton, Governor of Trinidad, for the torture of Luisa Calderon.

116 **Histoire de l'Ile de Trinidad sous le gouvernement espagnole.** (History of the island of Trinidad under the Spanish government.)
Pierre-Gustave-Louis Borde. Paris: Maisonneuve et Cie., 1876-1882. 2 vols.

This valuable work, based on considerable research, is one of the two major 19th-century histories of Trinidad. It covers the period from the Spanish discovery in 1498 to the British seizure of the island in 1797. The two volumes are heavily-footnoted and augmented with an appendix of important documents. Borde was a French resident and thus brings in much about the French settlers on the island.

117 **History of Trinidad.**
E. L. Joseph. Trinidad: H. J. Mills, 1838. Reprinted, London: Cass 1970. 272p. (Cass Library of West Indian Studies, no. 13).

Joseph's work, the second major 19th-century history of Trinidad, chronicles political developments up to 1837. Joseph was able to use now-destroyed Spanish records in writing this account, making it an important primary source for the pre-British period of Trinidad's history.

118 **A brief history of Trinidad under the Spanish crown.**
Claud Hollis. Port-of-Spain: A. L. Rhodes, M.B.E., 1941. 108p. bibliog.

Hollis was Governor of Trinidad and Tobago from 1930 to 1936. Drawing on published accounts, he traces the history of Trinidad from 1498 to 1797, covering Columbus, Walter Ralegh, attempts at colonization, European rivalries, the development of a cocoa industry, the Anglo-French War of 1793, and the capture of Trinidad by the British. Another brief history of the period is C. R. Ottley's *An account of life in Spanish Trinidad* (Port-of-Spain: College Press, 1955).

119 **An English library of Trinidad, 1633.**
Eleanor B. Adams. *The Americas*, vol. 12, no. 1 (July 1955), p. 25-41.

An account of the Spanish seizure of thirty-five secular books from an English group on Trinidad. The books were turned over to the Holy Office on the island of Margarita.

120 **The Couronians and the West Indies: the first settlements.**
Edgar Anderson. *Caribbean Quarterly*, vol. 5, no. 4 (June 1959), p. 264-71.

Anderson discusses the colonial settlements founded on Tobago by the Duchy of Courland, beginning in approximately 1634 and continuing until 1659-1660. The article is based on research in manuscript and printed sources.

121 **Foreign immigrants in Spanish America: Trinidad's colonisation experiment.**
Linda Newson. *Caribbean Studies*, vol. 19, nos. 1-2 (April-July 1979), p. 133-51.

In 1776 the Spanish Crown, for the first time in 200 years, actively encouraged foreigners to emigrate to Spanish America by offering concessions on Trinidad. Newson provides detailed information on this little studied aspect of Trinidad's history, discussing the economic stagnation of the island, Spain's colonization scheme, and the nature and impact of the foreign immigrants. Although the colonization project brought economic benefits to the island, its net result was that Trinidad became 'a French colony in all but name,' which led to unwelcome political consequences.

122 **The richest trade center of the Indies: a vision of Trinidad's future.**
Barbara Ifill. *Caribbean Quarterly*, vol. 10, no. 4 (Dec. 1964), p. 33-45.

An historical article on Spanish colonial Trinidad and its acquisition by the British in 1797.

Early British colonial period, 1797-1838

123 **A guide for the study of British Caribbean history, 1763-1834; including the abolition and emancipation movements.**
Lowell Joseph Ragatz. Washington, DC: Government Printing Office, 1932. 725p. (Annual Report of the American Historical Association, 1930, vol. 3).

This indispensible bibliographical guide for the period lists literature published before 1932, mainly concerning the years in the title, but in actuality going beyond these time boundaries. It covers all types of works, with both general sections and sections on specific islands, including Tobago, 'Documents,' p. 68-70; Trinidad, 'Documents,' p. 70-88; Tobago, 'Historical writings,' p. 205-06; and Trinidad, 'Historical writings,' p. 206-13. Other references to these islands can be reached through the index. Entries are provided with detailed, extremely informative annotations.

124 **Society and politics in colonial Trinidad.**
James Millette, with a foreword by Lewis E. Bobb. Curepe, Trinidad: Omega Bookshops; London: Zed Books, 1985. 295p. bibliog.

A reissue of Millette's *Genesis of crown colony government* (Curepe, Trinidad: Moko Enterprises, 1970). This is a history of Trinidad from 1783 to 1810, focussing on the administration of the conquered colony: 'it is the theory of this book that the period 1783 to 1810 in the history of Trinidad witnessed the genesis of the system of government known later as the Crown Colony system.' The volume's first chapter discusses the end of Spanish rule on the island.

125 **West Indian tales of old.**
Algernon E. Aspinall. London: Duckworth, 1915. Reprinted, New York: Negro Universities Press, 1969. 259p.

Among the historical episodes that the author retells is the story of 'Chaguaramas Bay, Trinidad,' an account of the incidents leading to the seizure of Trinidad by the British in 1797.

126 **Absentee landlordism in the British Caribbean, 1750-1833.**
Lowell J. Ragatz. *Agricultural History*, vol. 5, no. 1 (Jan. 1931), p. 7-24.

A scholarly article by a well-known historian. Ragatz discusses the forces that caused non-resident ownership to become the normal state of affairs in the British West Indies from the middle of the 18th century, a development in landholding that had disastrous consequences for the colonies. The volume deals with the West Indies as a whole. Ragatz is also the author of the classic study of the disintegration of the West Indian plantocracy, *The fall of the planter class in the British Caribbean, 1763-1833; a study in social and economic history* (New York: Century, 1928. Reprinted, London: Cass, 1963).

127 **The traffic in slaves between the British West Indian colonies, 1807-1833.**
D. Eltis. *Economic History Review*, second series, vol. 25, no. 1 (Feb. 1972), p. 55-64.

'Between 1807 and 1833 thousands of slaves were taken from the long-settled islands such as Barbados and Dominica and shipped to the newly acquired and much less developed colonies of Trinidad and Demerara.' Trinidad, which had net imports of slaves on a significant scale, figures largely in this article on the pre-emancipation West Indian inter-island slave trade, a subject on which little has been written.

128 **History of Trinidad.**
Lionel Mordaunt Fraser. Port-of-Spain: Government Printing House, 1891-96. Reprinted, London: Cass, 1971. 2 vols. (Cass Library of West Indian Studies, no. 20).

Except for the first two chapters, this is a history of the early British colonial period in Trinidad, to 1839. Volume one covers 1781 to 1813; volume two studies the period 1814 to 1839. The work is important for the official documents which Fraser includes, many of which have since been destroyed or are otherwise inaccessible.

129 **British colonial government after the American Revolution, 1782-1820.**
Helen Taft. New Haven, Connecticut: Yale University Press; London: Oxford University Press, 1933. 568p. bibliog. (Yale Historical Publications. Miscellany, no. 26).

A revision of the author's doctoral dissertation at Yale University in 1924. It is a scholarly study of 'the important developments in British colonial government for the years between Yorktown and the end of the Napoleonic era. . . . [This period] is perhaps the most obscure in the three and a quarter centuries of British colonization.' The work is based on research in primary resources, for the large part from documentary sources in the Public Records Office, London. Material on the governing and administration of Trinidad is included for the years after the island was acquired by the British in 1797. A bibliographical note on p. 541-68 evaluates the manuscript and unpublished sources used.

130 **A statistical, commercial, and political description of Venezuela, Trinidad, Margarita, and Tobago: containing various anecdotes and observations, illustrative of the past and present state of these interesting countries; from the French . . . with introd. and explanatory notes, by the editor.**
Jean Francois Dauxion-Lavayasse. London: G. & W. B. Whittaker, 1820. Reprinted, Westport, Connecticut: Negro Universities Press, 1969. 479p.

A translation of the author's *Voyage aux isles de Trinidad, de Tabago, de la Marguerite et dans diverses parties du Venezuela, dans l'Amérique méridionale* (Paris, 1813), adapted for the British public by having the French edition's anti-British remarks deleted. The volume presents firsthand observations of Trinidad, from 1792 to 1806.

131 **The Tobago slave conspiracy of 1801.**
K. O. Laurence. *Caribbean Quarterly*, vol. 28, no. 3 (Sept. 1982), p. 1-9. map.

Provides details of a slave conspiracy on the island of Tobago, where slaves plotted to rebel on a number of estates at Christmas, 1801. Their plans were discovered and their leaders arrested before the uprising could occur. The article is based on contemporary reports in the London Public Records Office.

132 **African and Creole slave family patterns in Trinidad.**
B. W. Higman. In: *Africa and the Caribbean; the legacies of a link.* Edited by Margaret E. Crahan, Franklin W. Knight. Baltimore, Maryland; London: Johns Hopkins University Press, 1979, p. 41-64.

'The hypothesis that the African heritage was of minor importance in shaping the family life of West Indian slaves has never been tested rigorously. . . . The necessary data are simply not available. . . . What is attempted here is an examination of the relationship between specific African origins and slave family structures in the island of Trinidad in 1813. This provides a picture of slave family life in the initial stages of the establishment of a plantation economy, the majority of the population being African-born.' The text of the article is enhanced by tables, including one of the ethnic/regional origins of Trinidad's African-born slaves in 1813, and a map of West and Central Africa, pinpointing the origins of the slaves.

133 **Some notes on Sir Ralph James Woodford, Bt. (Governor of Trinidad, 1813-1828).**
Gertrude Carmichael. *Caribbean Quarterly*, vol. 2, no. 3 (1951?), p. 26-38.

Woodford was appointed Governor of Trinidad in 1813 at the age of twenty-nine. He was the first civil governor, and he introduced many reforms and new measures for the improvement of the colony. Carmichael describes the policies of his administration in regard to land, settlement, labour, agriculture, slavery, the militia, finances, health concerns, the Church, schools, and the legal system.

134 **Domestic manners and social conditions of the white, coloured, and negro population of the West Indies.**
Mrs. [A. C.] Carmichael. London: Whittaker, Treacher & Co., 1833. Reprinted, New York: Negro Universities Press, 1969. 2 vols.

Mrs. Carmichael was a planter's wife who went to the West Indies in 1820 and spent five years in St. Vincent and Trinidad. Her anecdotes of domestic life on the plantations are informative, although her viewpoint is complacently racist and decidedly anti-emancipationist. Her years in Trinidad are covered in volume two.

135 **Some aspects of social structure in the British Caribbean about 1820.**
M. G. Smith. *Social and Economic Studies*, vol. 1, no. 4 (Aug. 1953), p. 55-80. bibliog.

Although Smith's analysis of early 19th-century West Indian society is based mainly on accounts describing pre-emancipation Jamaica and St. Vincent, he also mentions Trinidad, using Mrs. Carmichael's 1833 publication *Domestic manners and social conditions of the white, coloured and negro population of the West Indies* (q.v.) as his source. Smith identifies three main social strata in the West Indian society of the time, and sees each social section as practising a different culture.

136 **The slave family and household in the British West Indies, 1800 1834.**
B. W. Higman. *Journal of Interdisciplinary History*, vol. 6, no. 2 (Autumn 1975), p. 261-87.

Trinidad is included in this study of the slave family and slave household in the British Caribbean during the period after the abolition of the British slave trade in 1807 and before the abolition of slavery, in 1834. Demographic data on the constitution of the slave family in Trinidad is compared with similar data from Jamaica and Barbados. Higman concludes that 'the extent to which the different demographic histories of the slaves of the Caribbean and North America affected family and house-organization cannot be quantified satisfactorily at present. But it is apparent that the characterization of the slave family as matrifocal, unstable and promiscuous fits the Caribbean no better than North America. This conclusion has implications not only for the study of the family but for the understanding of slave society as a whole.' The article includes a table of family structure in Trinidad in 1813.

137 **Jonas Mohammed Bath and the free Mandingos in Trinidad: the question of their repatriation to Africa, 1831-1838.**
Carl Campbell. *Pan-African Journal*, vol. 7, no. 2 (Summer 1974), p. 129-52.

Bath, a man of some eminence in his native Africa, was taken as a slave to Trinidad in 1804 or 1805. There, in Port-of-Spain, he formed a society of Mandingo slaves who pooled their resources to purchase freedom for themselves and other Mandingos. Although the Port-of-Spain Mandingos prospered, they nevertheless wished to return to Africa. This article concerns their efforts to be repatriated by the British government and the Colonial Office's response. It is a thoroughly-documented account that sheds light on a little-known episode.

Middle British colonial period, 1838-1918

138 **Trinidad in transition; the years after slavery.**
Donald Wood. London, New York: Oxford University Press, for the Institute of Race Relations, 1968. 318p. map. bibliog.

Wood covers the middle years of the 19th century in Trinidad, from emancipation during the years 1834-1838 to the administration of Governor Arthur Gordon from 1866 to 1870. During this post-emancipation epoch, the newly-liberated and the dominant classes had to adapt to novel social conditions. These years saw the importation of indentured labourers to fill the vacancies on the plantations, conflicts between French and English cultural traditions on the island, and rivalries between the Anglican and the Roman Catholic churches.

139 **Observations on the present condition of the island of Trinidad, and the actual state of the experiment of Negro emancipation.**
William Hardin Burnley. London: Longman, Brown, Green & Longmans, 1842. 177p.

Burnley presents the planter's view of economic conditions after emancipation. As a Trinidadian slave-owner, he had led the fight against the government's attempts to ameliorate the lot of the slaves. After emancipation, he remained the spokesman for Trinidad's plantocracy.

140 **Kaye Dowland's book; a record of mid-19th century Tobago.**
David L. Niddrie. *Caribbean Quarterly*, vol. 9, no. 4 (Dec. 1963), p. 44-51.

A report on a manuscript in the Tobago Archives, Scarborough, entitled *Letter and returns 1843-1848* by Kaye Dowland. Dowland was appointed Special Magistrate in Tobago in 1835, with the task of overseeing the rights of emancipated slaves during the apprenticeship period. He continued to serve in various administrative capacities on the island until 1857.

141 **Trinidad: historical and descriptive; being a narrative of nine years residence in the island. With special reference to Christian missions.**
W. H. Gamble. London: Yates & Alexander, 1866. 120p.

A clergyman's view of mid-19th-century Trinidad.

142 **The experience of indentureship: 1845-1917.**
Bridget Brereton. In: *Calcutta to Caroni: the East Indians of Trinidad*. Edited by John Gaffar La Guerre. Port-of-Spain: Longmans Caribbean, 1974, p. 25-38.

A succinct summary of the setting and facts of indenture.

143 **A typology of the Caribbean peasantry – the development of the peasantry in Trinidad, 1845-1917.**
Raphael Sebastien. *Social and Economic Studies*, vol. 19, nos. 2 – 3 (June-Sept. 1980), p. 107-33.

An examination of agrarian development during a period of underdevelopment and backward capitalism in Trinidad. Sebastien constructs a categorization of the Trinidadian peasantry as 'pure' peasantry; peasant-farmer; and peasant-proletarian. The article traces the history of the peasantry and analyses the development of small cocoa cultivators and cane farmers.

144 **The impact of the Indian immigrants on colonial Trinidad society.**
Marianne D. Ramesar. *Caribbean Quarterly*, vol. 22, no. 1 (March 1976), p. 5-18.

Ramesar studies the effect which Indian immigration had on Trinidad's population size and composition, the nature of its social relationships, and its economic development from the mid-19th-century to the 1920s.

145 **East Indians and the larger society.**
Kevin Singh. In: *Calcutta to Caroni: the East Indians of Trinidad.* Edited by John Gaffar La Guerre. Port-of-Spain: Longmans Caribbean, 1974, p. 39-68.

This historico-sociological account traces the place that East Indians have held in Trinidadian society from 1845 to the mid-1970s.

146 **Sugar & East Indian indentureship in Trinidad.**
Ken I. Boodhoo. *Caribbean Review*, vol. 5, no. 2 (April-May-June 1973), p. 17-20.

This article emphasizes the importance of sugar in the political, economic, and social life of the British colony, and views the recruitment of East Indians to Trinidad as 'purely to further the development of a plantation-type sugar industry, which was controlled, directed and owned by British capital.' Boodhoo discusses the regulations under which the East Indians toiled, and notes that when the sugar industry was depressed in the late 19th century, the indentureship system was terminated.

147 **The East Indian indenture in Trinidad.**
Judith Ann Weller. Rio Piedras, Puerto Rico: Institute of Caribbean Studies, University of Puerto Rico, 1968. 172p. maps. bibliog. (Caribbean Monograph Series, no. 4).

A well-documented history of East Indian indenture from 1845 to 1917. The topics covered are: the system of recruitment; the passage overseas; the life of the migrants in Trinidad, (including both work and domestic arrangements); and repatriation to India. Governmental policies – British, West Indian, Indian, and Trinidadian – that affected the migrants are discussed, as is the campaign for the abolition of the indenture system.

148 **The career of Arthur Hamilton Gordon, first Lord Stanmore, 1829-1912.**
J. K. Chapman. Toronto: University of Toronto Press, 1964. 387p. bibliog.

Arthur Gordon was Governor of Trinidad from 1866 to 1870. During his administration, he dealt effectively with problems of land reform and education. Chapman's biography centres around Gordon's career as a colonial administrator.

149 **Coolie labor in Trinidad.**
Charles Kingsley. *Caribbean Review*, vol. 5, no. 2 (April-May-June 1973), p. 21-24.

This extract from Kingsley's *At last, a Christmas in the West Indies* gives the British novelist's observations on the East Indian workers that he saw in Trinidad in 1869-1870. He expresses a favourable view of the indenture system.

150 **Race relations in colonial Trinidad, 1870-1900.**
Bridget Brereton. Cambridge, England: Cambridge University Press, 1979. 251p. map. bibliog.

This very readable volume examines 'the nature of society and race relations in Trinidad in the last three decades of the nineteenth century, with special reference to the white, coloured, and black groups,' focusing on the gradual emergence of 'a non-white middle class . . . augmented from below.' Brereton comments that this development was crucial, 'for it was the coloured and black middle class which held the key to the political and social future of Trinidad.' The work includes chapters on the environment, the white élite, education and mobility, the rise of a coloured and black middle class, the urban labouring population, the black rural masses, the souls of black folk, the Indians, racism and race relations, and the divided society.

151 **Immigration and the sugar industry in Trinidad during the last quarter of the 19th century.**
Howard Johnson. *Journal of Caribbean History*, vol. 3 (Nov. 1971), p. 28-72.

Basing his views on research in government documents, Johnson reconsiders 'the contention of [some] writers on late 19th century Trinidad that there was a labour shortage in the colony.' Rather, he holds, 'a system [i.e. indentured Indian immigration] which had been of genuine benefit to the underpopulated colony by supplying a labour force in the years immediately following Emancipation served to depress the wages of the agricultural labourers by the 1880s.' Besides discussing the presumed labour shortage, Johnson covers the cost of immigration, the demand for migrant labour, the labour market in Trinidad from 1880 to 1897, and the attitudes of the colonial and metropolitan governments to the labour problem during these years.

152 **Henry Sylvester Williams: imperial Pan Africanist.**
J. R. Hooker. London: Collings, 1975. 135p.

A biography of Henry Sylvester Williams (1869-1911), the Trinidadian who was an initiator of the Pan-African movement. Besides providing biographical information on Williams, the book is informative on the intellectual climate of Trinidad before the First World War. Another biographical study of Williams is Owen C. Mathurin's *Henry Sylvester Williams and the origins of the Pan-African Movement, 1869-1911* (Westport, Connecticut: Greenwood, 1976).

153 **Child of the tropics: Victorian memoirs.**
Yseult Bridges, edited and completed by Nicholas Guppy. London: Collins, 1980. 205p.

Reminiscences of the author's childhood in Trinidad from 1890 to 1901.

154 **Toward a formulation of the Indian view of history: the representation of Indian opinion in Trinidad, 1900-1921.**
Gerad Tikasingh. In: *East Indians in the Caribbean; colonialism and the struggle for identity: papers presented to a symposium on East Indians in the Caribbean, the University of the West Indies, June, 1975.* Preface by Bridget Brereton, Winston Dookeran, with an introduction by V. S. Naipaul. Millwood, New York, London; Nendeln, Liechtenstein: Kraus International, 1982, p. 11-32.

This historical article details the East Indians' beliefs about their situation in Trinidad vis-à-vis the British and the Creoles: 'In Indian eyes, their contribution to the growth of the island's economy provided a bitter contrast to their disadvantaged position in the society.'

155 **The Trinidad Water Riots of 1903: reflections of an eye-witness.**
Edited by K. O. Laurence. *Caribbean Quarterly*, vol. 15, no. 4 (Dec. 1969), p. 5-22.

During the Water Riot of 23 March 1903, the old Red House was burnt down and most of the Government's records and papers destroyed. In this article, K. O. Laurence presents a manuscript written by Dr. Stephen Moister Laurence who had witnessed the early stages of the disturbance. Besides recounting the riot, Dr. Laurence reflects on some of the general characteristics of the system of Crown Colony government then in force in Trinidad. The article consists of the editor's introduction and notes and the text of the manuscript.

156 **Hugh Clifford in Trinidad, 1903-1907.**
A. J. Stockwell. *Caribbean Quarterly*, vol. 24, nos. 1-2 (March-June 1978), p. 8-33.

A historical article based on considerable research in archival sources. It provides details of the years that Hugh Clifford spent in Trinidad as Colonial Secretary, during which time he served for twelve months as the colony's governor.

157 **Cyrus Prudhomme David – a case study of the emergence of the black man in Trinidad politics.**
Brinsley Samaroo. *Journal of Caribbean History*, vol. 3 (Nov. 1971), p. 72-89.

'This article examines the career of one of Trinidad's first political agitators, who in 1904 became the first black member of its fully nominated Legislative Council, against the background of some of the restrictions under which the island's black population functioned.'

Late British colonial period, 1919-1962

158 **The British Caribbean; from the decline of colonialism to the end of Federation.**
Elisabeth Wallace. Toronto: University of Toronto Press, 1977. 274p. bibliog.

A history, coupled with a political analysis, of constitutional developments in twelve British Caribbean territories in the first six decades of the 20th century, up to the end of the West Indian Federation in 1962. There is much information on Trinidad and Tobago, as the country played a major role in the political evolution of the area.

159 **Black revolutionary: George Padmore's path from Communism to Pan-Africanism.**
James R. Hooker. New York: Praeger, 1967. 168p. bibliog. (Praeger Library of African Affairs).

A biography of the Black left-wing intellectual that chronicles his life and politics from his birth in Trinidad in 1902.

160 **Hercules and the Society of Peoples of African Origin.**
W. F. Elkins. *Caribbean Studies*, vol. 11, no. 4 (Jan. 1972), p. 47-59.

Although born in Venezuela, Felix Eugene Michael Hercules grew up in Trinidad and taught in San Fernando at Naparima College. After emigrating to Great

Britain, he became the editor of the London *African Telegraph* in 1918. In this article, Elkins discusses Hercules' support for the cause of British Blacks after the post-First World War anti-Black race riots in Liverpool and Cardiff. Hercules became the spokesman for what Elkins calls 'the most prosperous section of the weak West Indian national bourgeoisie,' and toured the West Indies, expounding his views.

161 **A source of Black nationalism in the Caribbean: the revolt of the British West Indies Regiment at Taranto, Italy.**
W. F. Elkins. *Science & Society*, vol. 34, no. 1 (Spring 1970), p. 99-103.

Elkins links the Trinidad longshoremen's strike of December 1919 with the revolt of the British West Indies Regiment that occurred at Taranto, Italy, in December 1918. He believes that black ex-soldiers supported the Trinidad strike because of their experiences in the revolt.

162 **Black power in the British West Indies: the Trinidad longshoremen's strike of 1919.**
W. F. Elkins. *Science & Society*, vol. 33, no. 1 (Winter 1969), p. 71-75.

Elkins views the stevedores' strike that took place in Port-of-Spain in November and December of 1919 as an early effusion of black nationalism.

163 **Revolutionary upheaval in Trinidad, 1919; views from British and American sources.**
Tony Martin. *Journal of Negro History*, vol. 58, no. 3 (July 1973), p. 313-26.

Traces the causes of the disturbances that broke out in Trinidad in December, 1919, and which offered a violent challenge to British colonial rule. The article includes interesting information on the American view of the incident.

164 **British policy toward a separate Indian identity in the Caribbean, 1920-1950.**
Hugh Tinker. In: *East Indians in the Caribbean; colonialism and the struggle for identity: papers presented to a symposium on East Indians in the Caribbean, the University of the West Indies, June, 1975.* Preface by Bridget Brereton, Winston Dookeran, with an introduction by V. S. Naipaul. Millwood, New York, London; Nendeln, Liechtenstein: Kraus International, 1982, p. 33-47.

'Among the many Indian communities overseas, those in the Caribbean (including Trinidad and Guyana) made the least impact upon British imperial policy. In their impact upon Indian opinion, they also seemed to be the least influential.'

165 **The role of the British Labour Movement in the development of labour organisation in Trinidad, 1929-1938.**
Sahadeo Basdeo. *Social and Economic Studies*, vol. 31, no. 1 (March 1982), p. 40-73. bibliog.

An informative study of a neglected aspect of the history of Trinidadian trade unionism. 'Between 1929 and 1938 the British Labour Movement exhibited great dynamism in Trinidad labour affairs. With the advent of the Second Labour Government the British Labour Movement was able to influence public policy towards labour and trade union organisation in the colonies, so much so that in September 1930 the famous "Passfield Memorandum" was passed encouraging the formation of constitutional trade unions in the colonial empire.'

166 **Butler versus the King: riots and sedition in 1937.**
Edited by W. Richard Jacobs, comments by George Weekes, Joe Young. Port-of-Spain: Key Caribbean Publications, 1976. 254p. bibliog.

Studies Uriah Butler and the oilfield disturbances that shook Trinidad in 1937.

167 **British West Indian reaction to the Italian-Ethiopian War: an episode of Pan-Africanism.**
Robert G. Weisbord. *Caribbean Studies*, vol. 10, no. 1 (April 1970), p. 34-51.

Includes an account of the response in Trinidad to the Italian aggression against Emperor Haile Selassie's kingdom, including comments on the invasion made at the time by Trinidadians George Padmore, C. L. R. James, and Eric Williams.

168 **The British grant of air and naval facilities to the United States in Trinidad, St. Lucia and Bermuda in June-December, 1939.**
F. A. Baptiste. *Caribbean Studies*, vol. 16, no. 2 (July 1976), p. 5-43.

'The purpose of this article is to throw some light on the British/American negotiations which led to the grant of the air and naval facilities in [Trinidad, Bermuda and St. Lucia] in 1939 and to suggest reasons why, after all, the facilities were not used by the United States.' The account is based on research in primary sources in Great Britain and the USA. The following documents pertaining to Trinidad are included in the appendixes: 'Re the original Trinidad lease' and 'Proposed amendments to the original Trinidad lease.'

169 **The general elections of 1946 in Trinidad and Tobago.**
John Gaffar La Guerre. *Social and Economic Studies*, vol. 21, no. 2 (June 1972), p. 184-204.

'This paper is mainly descriptive. It deals with the first general election to be held in Trinidad and Tobago under adult suffrage; it identifies some of the social forces that had begun to emerge and which would still dominate the politics of Trinidad; and relates them to some of the theoretical issues of West Indian politics.' Appendix one lists the slates of parties and candidates that took part in the 1946 election; and Appendix two provides a breakdown of the population of Trinidad and Tobago in 1946 by race.

170 **The race factor and the election of 1950 in Trinidad and Tobago.**
John Gaffar LaGuerre. *Social and Economic Studies*, vol. 29, nos. 2-3 (July-Sept. 1980), p. 321-35. bibliog.

A well-documented study of the impact of race on the General Election of 1950, which comments that 'A most significant consequence of the 1950 election was that it demonstrated the powerful presence of East Indians in the politics of Trinidad and Tobago.' LaGuerre also notes the relationship of race to other factors in Trinidadian politics of the time.

171 **The Trinidad and Tobago General Election of 1961.**
Gordon K. Lewis. *Caribbean Studies*, vol. 2, no. 2 (July 1962), p. 2-30.

Describes the electoral battle of 1961, which confirmed Eric Williams's People's National Movement in power. Lewis provides a close analysis of Trinidadian political groupings shortly before independence.

The Federation of the West Indies, 1958-1962

172 **The rise and demise of the Federation of the West Indies.**
F. A. Barrett. *Canadian Review of Studies in Nationalism*, vol. 1, no. 2 (Spring 1974), p. 248-54.

A short history of the Federation of the West Indies, from the time it was first bruited in 1945 to its demise in 1962. This article has been reprinted in Roberta Marx Delson, ed., *Readings in Caribbean history and economics; an introduction to the region* (New York, London, Paris: Gordon & Breach, 1981, p. 292-99).

173 **Federation of the West Indies.**
Sir John Mordecai. Evanston, Illinois: Northwestern University Press, 1968. 484p. map. bibliog.

An oft-cited study of the negotiations that led to federation among the islands of the British Caribbean in 1958. 'This book is a history of the agitation for Federation, of negotiations over forty years, of rabid differences, some of them specious, dividing great island leaders, of the compromises upon which the Federation was founded and of its dramatic failure after four fractious years.' In an epilogue, W. Arthur Lewis discusses the reasons behind the break-up of the West Indian Federation in 1962.

174 **The federal principle in the British West Indies: an appraisal of its use.**
Lewis E. Bobb. *Social and Economic Studies*, vol. 15, no. 3 (Sept. 1966), p. 239-65.

An excellent presentation of both the history of and the political thinking behind the thrust for federation in the British Caribbean, which resulted in the Federation of the West Indies that existed from 3 January 1958 to 29 May 1962. Bobb comments that 'the federalism tried in the West Indies was of classical Anglo-American kind. It was therefore shaped in rigidities – legal, individualist, and self-regarding. . . . [This] legalistic approach to federation . . . prevented that flexibility needed to overcome economic rigidities.'

175 **West Indies Federation: perspectives on a new nation.**
Edited by David Lowenthal. New York: Columbia University Press in cooperation with the Geographical Society and Carleton University, 1961. 142p. map. bibliog. (American Geographical Society Research Series, no. 23).

The editor and three other Caribbean specialists – H. W. Springer, Gordon Merrill, and Douglas G. Anglin – contribute individual essays on social and political topics at the time when ten West Indian territories – Jamaica, Trinidad and Tobago, Barbados, Grenada, St. Vincent, St. Lucia, Dominica, Antigua, St. Kitts-Nevis-Anguilla, and Montserrat – had joined in the West Indian Federation. A valuable addition to the text is Lowenthal's annotated thirty-five page bibliography, 'A selected West Indian reading list.'

Independent Trinidad and Tobago, 1962-.

176 **Eric Williams: the man and the leader.**
Edited by Ken I. Boodhoo. Lanham, Maryland: University Press of America, 1986. 162p.

Described in its publisher's catalogue as 'the first in-depth analysis and appraisal of the contributions to Caribbean society by Eric Williams. . . . [Includes] a psychological profile of Eric Williams' mystical personality, [a] survey of his economic ideas as they were reflected in state economic policies, and an appraisal of him as a scholar. . . . Also includes personal insights by Dr. Williams' daughter, Erica Williams.'

177 **Eric Williams, leader of Trinidad and Tobago, is dead.**
C. Gerald Fraser. *New York Times* (31 March 1981), p. D22.

An obituary of the historian and politician who led his two-island nation to independence. It provides a summary of Williams's career and his scholarly and political achievements.

178 **Trinidad and Tobago: international perspectives.**
Eric Williams. *Freedomways*, vol. 4, no. 3 third quarter, (Summer 1964), p. 331-40.

A tribute to Trinidad and Tobago by its then Prime Minister. Dr. Williams contrasts his nation with other Caribbean states, characterizing Trinidad as an independent country in a modern world. He points out that in Trinidad there is an active partnership between government and investors, and direct democracy within a parliamentary tradition.

179 **Trinidad and Tobago.**
Eric Williams. *Current History*, vol. 56, no. 329 (Jan. 1969), p. 47-49; 54.

Dr. Williams who was then Prime Miniter of Trinidad and Tobago, sketches the economic problems of the newly-independent nation and outlines his government's goals for the economy as Trinidad prepared to embark on its third five-year economic plan.

180 **An analysis of the general elections in Trinidad and Tobago, 1971.**
Edward Greene. In: *Readings in government and politics of the West Indies.* Edited by Trevor Munroe, Rupert Lewis. Mona, Jamaica: Dept. of Government, University of the West Indies, 1971, p. 136-45.

Provides political analysis of the 1971 elections.

181 **Trinidad and Tobago: the general elections of 1976.**
Selwyn D. Ryan. *Caribbean Studies*, vol. 19, nos. 1-2 (April-July 1979), p. 5-32.

An examination by a political scientist of the political parties, including the People's National Movement and the Democratic Action Congress, candidates, campaign, and results of the 1976 General Elections. Ryan's discussion is particularly interesting for its analysis of the radical United Labour Front (ULF) party.

Population and Nationalities

20th century

182 **The population of Trinidad and Tobago.**
Jack Harewood. Paris: Committee for International Coordination of National Research in Demography, 1975. 237p. (CICRED Series).

A thorough discussion of the economically active population of the nation from 1891 to the 1960s. Harewood is also the author of *Population projections for Trinidad and Tobago, 1970-2000* (Port-of-Spain: Institute for Social and Economic Research, University of the West Indies, 1978).

183 **Fertility and mating in four West Indian populations: Trinidad and Tobago, Barbados, St. Vincent, Jamaica.**
George W. Roberts, with an introduction by D. V. Glass. Mona, Jamaica: Institute of Social and Economic Research, University of the West Indies, 1975. 341p. bibliog.

'An analysis of fertility and mating patterns as revealed in the 1960 population censuses of Jamaica, Trinidad and Tobago, Barbados and St. Vincent and relevant vital statistics. Findings from surveys conducted in Trinidad and Barbados are also drawn on.'

184 **1970 Population Census.**
Central Statistical Office. Port-of-Spain: Population Census Division, C.S.O., 1971- .

A multi-volume report of the 1970 Trinidad and Tobago Population Census.

185 **Population growth in Trinidad and Tobago in the twentieth century.**
Jack Harewood. *Social and Economic Studies*, vol. 12, no. 1 (March 1963), p. 1-26.

Trinidad and Tobago's population increased by 203 per cent between 1901 and 1960, rising from 275,000 to 828,000. Harewood analyses census figures to isolate current trends in the islands' population growth. The inclusion of vital statistics in easily grasped tabular form adds to the article's usefulness.

186 **The Indian population in Trinidad and Tobago.**
Mukul D. Dey. *International Journal of Comparative Sociology*, vol. 3, no. 2 (Dec. 1962), p. 245-53.

This article provides 'demographic analyses of Indian vs. non-Indian populations. Indians have increased at a considerably greater rate than non-Indians, 1851-1946, due to a greater natural increase. The proportions of Indians in the population rose from 5.28% in 1851 to 36.88% in 1946.'

187 **Race and population patterns in Trinidad.**
John P. Augelli, Harry W. Taylor. *Annals of the Association of American Geographers*, vol. 50, no. 2 (June 1960), p. 123-38.

An interesting article on Trinidad's population which the authors term the 'most heterogeneous in the West Indies.' After an overview of its origins, the authors cover the distribution of the population and racial patterns in 1959, then go on to discuss the island's cultural diversity as evinced in its geographical names, architecture, linguistic influences, and social stratification. Illustrated with photographs, the article also includes maps showing population distribution (1959), relief patterns (1959), land use (1950), racial patterns (1946 modified), and selected place-names.

188 **Population and Vital Statistics; Report.**
Port-of-Spain: Central Statistical Office, 1953- . annual.

This compilation of basic demographic data covers population by size and structure, population growth, birth rate, mortality rate, marriages and divorces.

Pre-20th century

189 **The settlement of free Negroes in Trinidad before emancipation.**
K. O. Laurence. *Caribbean Quarterly*, vol. 9, nos. 1-2 (1963), p. 26-52.

A scholarly, well documented essay on 'two attempts . . . to settle in Trinidad negro troops who had served in the British forces [during the Napoleonic Wars] together with a few other free negroes for whom Britain had been responsible.' Maps show the location of the settlements at Naparima and at Manzanilla and Quare described in the article.

190 **The Chinese in Trinidad, 1806-1838.**
B. W. Higman. *Caribbean Studies*, vol. 12, no. 3 (Oct. 1972), p. 21-44.

'The idea that a settlement of Chinese should be attempted in Trinidad seems to have originated with William Layman, a captain of the Royal Navy . . . in 1802.' The Colonial Office favoured the plan and recruitment of Chinese from Southeast Asia began in 1803-1804. The first Chinese arrived in Trinidad on 12 October 1806. This article describes the economic and social activities of these pioneer free Asiatic settlers. The experiment was not considered successful as far as white expectations of procuring a class of free plantation labourers went, since few Chinese were interested in remaining on the plantations. The plan was not pursued at the time, but after Emancipation, the Chinese were again considered as candidates for immigration to Trinidad by the English.

191 **Summary statistics on indenture and associated migration affecting the West Indies, 1834-1918.**
G. W. Roberts, J. Byrne. *Population Studies*, vol. 20, no. 1 (July 1966), p. 125-34.

Useful tables bring together statistics on migration into the British Caribbean (including Trinidad) from India, Madeira, Africa, China, Europe, and other parts of the world. The authors discuss and evaluate the sources from which the statistics presented here were drawn.

192 **Immigration of Africans into the British Caribbean.**
G. W. Roberts. *Population Studies*, vol. 7, no. 3 (March 1954), p. 235-62.

This thorough presentation of the facts of African immigration into the Caribbean area during the period 1841 to 1867, furnishes information on the flow of free Black settlers to Trinidad. 'African immigration to Trinidad (excluding Tobago) up to 1861 amounted to 8300, while those returning to Africa during the same period numbered 2700.' An appendix provides a discussion of the statistical sources upon which Roberts based his figures and conclusions.

193 **Patterns of regional settlement and economic activity by immigrant groups in Trinidad: 1851-1900.**
Marianne Ramesar. *Social and Economic Studies*, vol. 25, no. 3 (Sept. 1976), p. 187-215. maps. bibliog.

In this painstaking work, Ramesar traces emerging patterns of settlement in 19th-century Trinidad by the two main immigrant groups – the British West Indians and the East Indians. 'Available quantitative data, especially from population censuses for the years 1851-1901, is used to corroborate the observations of contemporary eye-witnesses.'

Emigration

General

194 **The outflow of trained personnel from Trinidad and Tobago.**
Leo Pujadas. In: *The brain drain from five developing countries: Cameroon – Colombia – Lebanon – the Phillipines – Trinidad and Tobago.* United Nations Social Development Division. New York: United Nations Institute for Training and Research, 1971, p. 42-66. (UNITAR Research Reports, no. 5).

Pujadas emphasizes the costs of the emigration of trained personnel from Trinidad and Tobago.

195 **Report of a Cabinet-appointed enquiry into discrimination against nationals of Trinidad and Tobago in the United Kingdom, Canada and the United States of America.**
Clive Spencer. Port-of-Spain: Government Printery, 1969. 32p. (Trinidad and Tobago. Senate Paper, no. 7 of 1969).

A report to the Trinidad and Tobago Senate on problems faced by Trinidadian emigrants abroad.

Emigration to Great Britain and Trinidadians in Great Britain

196 **West Indian migration to Great Britain; a social geography.**
Ceri Peach. London, New York: Oxford University Press for the Institute of Race Relations, 1968. 122p. maps.

A short work dealing with Commonwealth immigrants in the United Kingdom.

197 **Black British: immigrants to England.**
R. B. Davison. London: Oxford University Press for the Institute of Race Relations, 1966. 170p.

A study of black emigrants from the Commonwealth, including the Caribbean, and the strains and stresses of their interactions with native Britons.

198 **West Indian migrants; social and economic facts of migration from the West Indies.**
R. B. Davison, with a foreword by A. D. Knox. London, New York: Oxford University Press for the Institute of Race Relations, 1962. 89p. bibliog.

Davison concentrates on the economic conditions of the West Indian emigrants in the United Kingdom. This book first appeared as an article in the *West Indian Economist* (July-Oct. 1961).

Emigration to the USA and Trinidadians in the USA

199 **Black immigration and ethnicity in the United States: an annotated bibliography.**
Center for Afroamerican and African Studies, University of Michigan. Westport, Connecticut; London: Greenwood Press, 1985. 170p. (Bibliographies and Indexes in Afro-American and African Studies, no. 2).

The main body of this work covers materials dealing with the immigration of peoples of African descent, both from the Caribbean area and directly from the African continent, to the United States. Included are bibliographies, literature surveys, general works on immigration and ethnicity, and United States immigration legislation and policies. Materials on the Trinidadians can be found in section three, part five 'West Indians,' which is classified by immigrant groups. Roughly one-half of the entries in the volume are annotated. Section six is a 'Select list of works on Black immigration to Canada and Great Britain.'

200 **Migration and sex roles: a comparison of Black and Indian Trinidadians in New York City.**
Judith Burgess, Meryl James-Gray. In: *Female immigrants to the United States.* Edited by D. M. Mortimer, R. S. Bryce-Laporte. Washington, DC: Smithsonian Institution, Research Institute on Immigration and Ethnic Studies, 1981, p. 85-111. (Occasional Papers, no. 2).

'This study is based on interviews with 28 Trinidadian women in New York City. Comparisons are made between Black and Indian Trinidadians in respect to three variables as they are affected by the immigration experience: (1) social mobility and economic attainment, (2) racial minority identification, and (3) changes in sex role and family relationship.'

201 **West Indians and Afro-Americans.**
Lennox Raphael. *Freedomways*, vol. 4, no. 3 (Summer 1964, Third Quarter), p. 445-51.

An article by a Trinidadian on the West Indian experience in the United States in the early 1960s, focusing particularly on West Indian relations with American Blacks. Raphael touches on the friction existing between the two groups, and calls on them to make an effort to understand one another. Mention is made in the article of West Indian immigrants, including Trinidadians, who have become well-known in the United States.

202 **'Well caught, Mr. Holder!'**
J. M. Flagler. *New Yorker*, vol. 30 (25 Sept. 1954), p. 65ff.

'A Reporter at Large' feature article. Flagler's account of West Indian cricket and cricketers in New York City in 1954 is delightful. It includes mention of Trinidadians.

Internal migration

203 **A demographic analysis of internal migration in Trinidad and Tobago; a descriptive and theoretical orientation.**
Joy M. Simpson. Mona, Jamaica: Institute of Social and Economic Research, University of the West Indies, 1973. 63p.

'A descriptive analysis of internal migration in Trinidad and Tobago between 1931 and 1960. Migration streams and characteristics are highlighted.'

Folklore

General

204 **Afro-American folk culture: an annotated bibliography of materials from North, Central, and South America, and the West Indies.**
John F. Szwed, Roger D. Abrahams, with Robert Baron (et al). Philadelphia: Institute for the Study of Human Issues, 1978. 2 vols. (Publications of the American Folklore Society. Bibliographical and Special Series, vols. 31-32).

The arrangement of this bibliography is geographical, with indexes by both broad subject and locale. The English-speaking West Indies section in the second volume includes material on Trinidad and Tobago. Bibliographical details and short annotations describe books and periodical articles to 1973. Forty-nine journals in the folklore field were scanned for this bibliography.

205 **The shaping of folklore traditions in the British West Indies.**
Roger D. Abrahams. *Journal of Inter-American Studies*, vol. 9, no. 3 (July 1967), p. 456-80.

An informative background discussion of the historical, geographical, ecological, social, and economic factors that affected the formation and perpetuation of West Indian folklore as a whole, coupled with an analysis of the aesthetic patterns and forces that can be discerned in West Indian folklore. Examples of Trinidadian folklore are referred to.

206 **Mermaids and fairymaids or water gods and goddesses of Tobago.**
H. B. Meikle. *Caribbean Quarterly*, vol. 5, no. 2 (Feb 1958), p. 103-08.

This article provides information on the 'water people' of Tobago, describing their appearance, habits, and habitats, and relating the stories told and the beliefs held about them by the local people. It is interesting to note that a 'mermaid' in Tobagonian tradition is male, the 'fairymaid' being his female counterpart.

207 **Folklore in Trinidad.**
Olga Comma. In: *Negro anthology, 1931-1933*. Edited by Nancy Cunard. London: Wishart, 1934. Reprinted, New York: Negro Universities Press, 1969, p. 486-88.

Describes Trinidadian folk beliefs and customs, including *maljo*, and gives an example of one of the island's folk-tales.

208 **Folk-lore of the Antilles, French and English.**
Elsie Clews Parsons. New York: Stechert, for the American Folklore Society, 1933-42. 3 vols. (Current Memoirs of the American Folklore Society, vol. 26, pts. 1-3).

In Part one, p. 1-70, there are fifty-eight folk-tales in English and French Creole that Parsons collected from informants in Trinidad. In Part three, p. 363-68, are sixty-seven riddles from Trinidad and on p. 457-58, sixteen proverbs. The Trinidad tales are also included in 'Summaries of the tales with bibliographical references' (Part three, p. 15-336).

209 **The evil-eye and related beliefs in Trinidad.**
James Hornell. *Folk-Lore*, vol. 35, no. 3 (Sept. 1924), p. 270-75.

Trinidadians call the evil-eye *maljo*, a corruption of the Spanish term *mal de ojo*; it is also sometimes called *hoodoo*. Hornell describes precautions taken against this malign magical practice. He also discusses beliefs about other objects and acts that are considered lucky or unlucky by the island's inhabitants.

Proverbs

210 **Tobago villagers in the mirror of dialect.**
H. B. Meikle. *Caribbean Quarterly*, vol. 4, no. 2 (Dec. 1955), p. 154-60.

A non-scholarly article that emphasizes the colourfulness of the Tobago dialect, as expressed in the islanders' proverbs. Meikle quotes and explains many Tobagonian sayings, as well as listing others that need no explanation.

211 **Trinidad proverbs ('old time sayings so').**
Melville J. Herskovits. *Journal of American Folklore*, vol. 58, no. 229 (July-Sept. 1945), p. 195-207.

Proverbs collected by Herskovits in the village of Toco, northeastern Trinidad, in 1939. The sayings were intended to be included in Elsie Clews Parsons' *Folklore of the Antilles, French and English* (q.v.), and correspond to those published on p. 457-87 of that book. Parsons' death prevented their inclusion, but, where possible, Herskovits keys these proverbs to those in the publication. One hundred and fifty-one proverbs are listed with first the saying in Creole dialect, then an explanation of its meaning.

Folk medicine

212 **Creole and doctor medicine: folk beliefs, practices, and orientations to modern medicine in a rural and an industrial suburban setting in Trinidad and Tobago, the West Indies.**
William R. Aho, Kimlan Minott. *Social Science and Medicine*, vol. 11, no. 5 (March 1977), p. 349-55.

'Based on interviews conducted during 1974 and 1975 with seventy-seven mothers in Trinidad, data are presented on their beliefs about childhood illnesses and attitudes toward "doctor medicine." The hot-cold system of classifying illness and cures is described, and one supernatural illness and its treatment by traditional healers – maljo. Data from interviews with two traditional healers and two district health nurses are also included. . . . Some implications of the study for health education and health care providers are discussed.'

213 **Folk medicine in Trinidad.**
George E. Simpson. *Journal of American Folklore*, vol. 75, no. 298 (Oct.-Dec. 1962), p. 326-40.

A highly detailed presentation of the therapeutic practices of Shango cultists and Shouters (Spiritual Baptists). Simpson covers the folk theory of sickness, folk practitioners, and the relation of the Shango 'powers' to healing. He lists the materials used in healing and conjuring: leaves, flowers, grasses, barks, roots, seeds, pods, fruits, vegetables, oils and perfumes, drugs, and miscellaneous accessories. After describing remedies, formulas, and rituals, Simpson ends his article with a discussion of changes (as of the early 1960s) in Trinidadian folk healing practices, and notes a decline in the use of folk medicine on the island.

214 **Faith healing and medical practice in the southern Caribbean.**
Frances Mischel. *Southwestern Journal of Anthropology*, vol. 15, no. 4 (Winter 1959), p. 407-17.

Mischel contrasts 'bush' or faith healing with legitimate medical practice on the islands of Trinidad and Grenada, where healing is a major function of Afro-

American cult leaders. Mischel interviewed six medical practitioners in Trinidad, contrasting their standard medical treatments with those meted out by faith healers or 'bush doctors.' She describes typical Shango healing ceremonies and cures by faith healers. The article ends with some interesting comments on the positive value attached to illness in Trinidadian society.

Folk-tales

215 **Mouth open, jump out.**
Grace Hallworth. London: Methuen Children's, 1984. 112p.

An anthology of Trinidadian tales and legends for children.

216 **Folk tales and fantasies.**
Michael Anthony. Port-of-Spain: Columbus Publishers, 1976. 65p.

Folk-tales selected by a Trinidadian novelist.

217 **Ma Rose Point: an anthology of rare and strange legends from Trinidad and Tobago.**
J. D. Elder. Port-of-Spain: National Cultural Council of Trinidad and Tobago, 1972. 79p.

An intriguingly-titled collection of eighteen legends and folk-tales, which includes musical transcriptions of songs mentioned in the stories.

218 **Folk stories and legends of Trinidad.**
M. P. Alladin. Trinidad: C.S.O. Printing Unit, 1968. 27p.

Ten folk stories and legends.

219 **Black gods, green islands.**
Geoffrey Holder, Tom Harshman. Garden City, New York: Doubleday, 1959. 235p.

The first tale in this volume, 'Papa Bois,' is based on the African folklore of Trinidad.

220 **A Trinidad Hindi riddle tale.**
Daniel J. Crowley. *Caribbeana*, vol. 9, no. 2 (Sept. 1955), p. 28 ff.

A rare piece of Trinidad's East Indian folklore.

221 **Tobago legends and West Indian lore.**
C. R. Ottley. Georgetown: Daily Chronicle, 1950. 137p.

Ottley is also the author of *True tales of Trinidad and Tobago* (Port-of-Spain: 1972), which consists of nineteen legends and historical tales from the islands.

Folk-music

General

222 **Music in Caribbean popular culture.**
Andrew Pearse. *Revista/Review Interamericana*, vol. 8, no. 4 (Winter 1978-79), p. 629-39.

A unique discussion of the musical culture of the non-élite classes in the islands of Trinidad, Tobago, Grenada, and Carriacou. Pearse traces the evolution of popular music from the post-emancipation period of the 1830s up to the 1950s – the time when commercial, mechanically reproduced music began to have an influence in the islands. After a broad overview of the region's musical culture, sections on music and social institutions list the different kinds of music performed, providing the local name for each type. Of the thirty-one types of music listed, at least twenty-one are connected in some way with Trinidad and/or Tobago.

223 **Color, music, and conflict: a study of aggression in Trinidad with reference to the role of traditional music.**
J. D. Elder. In: *Black society in the New World.* Edited by Richard Frucht. New York: Random House, 1971, p. 315-23. bibliog.

Elder views Trinidadian folk music from a unique psychological perspective.

Steelbands

224 **From Congo drum to steelband: a socio-historical account of the emergence and evolution of the Trinidad steel orchestra.**
J. D. Elder. St. Augustine, Trinidad: University of the West Indies, 1969. 47p.

A history of Trinidad's unique musical ensemble, the steelband.

225 **Steelbands: a personal record.**
Landeg E. White. *Caribbean Quarterly*, vol. 15, no. 4 (Dec. 1969), p. 32-39.

A non-Trinidadian musician details his personal experience of playing in a Trinidad steelband, the Scherzando Steelband from Tunapuna.

226 **The saga of the steelband.**
Donald R. Hanson, Robert Dash. *Caribbean*, vol. 8, no. 8 (March 1955), p. 173 ff.

A modest but nicely-detailed sketch of Trinidad's steelbands. The authors trace the steel drum back to its origin in the bamboo-tamboo of the 1890s. Another short article on the evolution of Trinidad's steel ensembles is Percival Borde's 'The sounds of Trinidad: the development of the steel drum bands' in *Black Perspective in Music*, vol. 2, no. 1 (Spring 1973), p. 45-49.

Steelbands – recordings

227 **Steel band.**
New York: Folkways Records and Service Corporation, 1957. [Sound recording]. (Folkways 6865).

A recording of the Trinidad Panharmonic Orchestra.

Folk-songs

228 **Song games from Trinidad and Tobago.**
J. D. Elder. N.p.: *American Folklore Society*, 1965, c.1962. 119p. bibliog. (Publications of the American Folklore Society. Bibliographical and Special Series, v. 16).

A collection of children's song-games gathered by Elder on Trinidad and Tobago. The volume comprises thirty games, providing verses, music, and instructions for playing. Elder's forty-nine page introduction is a study of the song-game as a specific folklore genre. A short discography lists available recordings.

229 **Songs from Trinidad.**

Edric Connor. London: Oxford University Press, 1958. 76p.

A volume of selected folk-songs. Another collection of Trinidadian songs is M. P. Alladin's *Folk chants and refrains of Trinidad and Tobago* (Port-of-Spain: CSO, 1969).

230 **Songs of a Rada community in Trinidad.**

Alan P. Merriam, Sara Whinery, B. G. Fred. *Anthropos*, vol. 51 (1956), p. 157-74.

A highly technical analysis of the songs sung by a Rada cult group in Port-of-Spain, as recorded by Andrew Carr in 1953. The paper deals first with the structural characteristics of the songs, then compares the Rada music with other New World Black and African songs. Three specimens of the songs in musical notation accompany the article.

Calypso

231 **Kaiso! the Trinidad calypso: a study of the calypso as oral literature.**
Keith Q. Warner. Washington, DC: Three Continents, 1982. 2nd rev. ed. 165p. bibliog.

A recent study of Trinidad's calypso music from its origins down to the present. Warner's focus is on the language of the form, covering male-female interplay, fantasy and humour, and social and political content in calypso lyrics. Two complete scores of calypso songs are included: the Mighty Sparrow's 'Welcome to Trinidad,' and Shadow's 'Sugar plum calypso.' The volume also includes a discography of calypso recordings.

232 **Leon Damas and the calypso.**
Keith Q. Warner. *CLA Journal*, vol. 19, no. 3 (March 1976), p. 374-81.

Investigates the affinities between the calypso and the poems of the French Guyanese poet Leon Damas. While Damas is not a calypsonian, formal elements from the Trinidadian calypso are utilized in his work.

233 **Gordon Rohlehr's 'Sparrow and the language of calypso.'**
[Edward Brathwaite, Gordon Rohlehr.] *Caribbean Quarterly*, vol. 14, nos. 1-2 (March-June 1968), p. 91-96.

Brathwaite and Rohlehr discuss the metric organization of speech rhythm as used by the calypsonian 'Sparrow' in his calypso lyrics.

234 **A history of neo-African literature: writing in two continents.**
Janheinz Jahn, translated from the German by Oliver Coburn, Ursula Lehrburger. London: Faber, 1968. 301p. bibliog.

In this history of the literature written by Africans both in Africa and in the Americas, Jahn includes a brief section on calypso. He quotes two Trinidadian calypsoes by 'Young Growler': 'The too foot santipead' and 'The story of lion's lost watch.'

235 **One hundred and twenty calypsoes to remember.**
Slinger Francisco ['Mighty Sparrow']. Port-of-Spain: National Recording Company, 1963. 92p.

Noteworthy examples of the calypso genre are brought together by Trinidad's most famous calypsonian, the 'Mighty Sparrow.'

236 **Toward a definition of calypso, part 1.**
Daniel J. Crowley. *Ethnomusicology*, vol. 3, no. 2 (May 1959), p. 57-66.

The study is continued in 'Toward a definition of calypso, part 2,' in *Ethnomusicology*, vol. 3, no. 3 (Sept. 1959), p. 117-23. Crowley is also the author of 'Calypso: Trinidad carnival songs and dances' in *Dance Notation Record*, vol. 9, no. 2 (1958), p. 3-7.

237 **Mitto Sampson on calypso legends of the nineteenth century.**
Mitto Sampson, arranged and edited by Andrew Pearse. *Caribbean Quarterly*, vol. 4, nos. 3-4 (March-June 1956) p. 250-62.

The text of this article has been complied from typescripts and recorded interviews with Mitto Sampson, a Trinidad polemic writer and Port-of-Spain character. An amateur folklorist, '[Sampson] has spent a great deal of his time in tracking down truth and legend, often inextricably mixed, about the underworld of Trinidad.' This is an extremely interesting and informative collection of legends of the exploits of calypsonians and of the calypso milieu, and includes quotations from calypso verses.

238 **Whence came the calypso.**
Alton A. Adams. *Caribbean*, vol. 8, no. 10 (May 1955), p. 218-20; 230; 235.

A short journalistic piece on West Indian Black folk-music, distinguishing it from art music. Adams traces the West Indian dance to African drum beat rhythmic patterns. He states that the 'origin of the name calypso . . . remains a mystery.'

239 **Trinidad calypso is unique folk culture.**
Andrew Carr. *Caribbean Commission Monthly Information Bulletin*, vol. 7, no. 7 (Feb. 1954), p. 162-64.

In this popular article, Carr, a folklore scholar, defines calypso, traces the etymology of its name, and also provides a history of the form. Mention is made of the imaginative and grandiose sobriquets adopted by calypso singers as 'noms de pièce,' and the inspiration for calypso lyrics – Trinidad's politics, international and local events – is discussed. Carr quotes from calypso lyrics to illustrate the realistic banter which is characteristic of the form.

240 **Trinidad calypso not unique.**
E. Jourdain. *Caribbean Commission Monthly Information Bulletin*, vol. 7, no. 10 (May 1954), p. 221-22.

A reply to Andrew Carr's article 'Trinidad calypso is unique folk culture' (q.v.). Jourdain posits a French origin for such Trinidad customs as calypso and carnival.

241 **Land of the calypso; the origin and development of Trinidad's folk song.**
Charles S. Espinet, Harry Pitts. Port-of-Spain: Guardian Commercial Printery, 1944. 74p.

Although this work deals mainly with the calypso – the authors attribute the origin of the form to African, French, and Spanish sources, and trace its history from 1898 – other types of Trinidadian folk-music and dance are also discussed. Includes text and music for calypsoes.

Calypso recordings

242 **Jump up carnival in Trinidad. [Sound recording].**
Emory Cook. Stamford, Connecticut: Cook Laboratories, [n.d.]. Cook 1072. 33⅓ rpm. microgroove. 1 12 in. disc.

This is a recording of an actual calypso carnival that took place in Port-of-Spain. The recording includes the following calypsoes: 'Steelband pageant'; 'Calypso talent'; 'Carib jazz'; 'Taxi driver'; 'Winning the calypso crown'; 'Tenor pan tuning.' The record is accompanied by programme notes by Emory Cook.

Festivals

243 **The Hindu festival of Divali in the Caribbean.**
J. C. Jha. *Caribbean Quarterly*, vol. 22, no. 1 (March 1976), p. 53-61.

Jha describes how Hinduism's great autumn festival, Divali, the Festival of Lights, is celebrated by East Indians in Trinidad, where it is an official national holiday. The article gives a meticulously detailed presentation of the rituals of the feast.

244 **African feasts in Trinidad.**
Maureen Warner. *Bulletin of the African Studies Association of the West Indies*, vol. 4 (Dec. 1971), p. 85-94.

Describes late-19th and early-20th-century African celebrations in Trinidad. Both religious and secular feasts are included.

245 **East Indian festivals in Trinidad life.**
Daniel J. Crowley. *Caribbean Commission Monthly Information Bulletin*, vol. 7, no. 9 (April 1954), p. 202-08.

In this article, Crowley, an anthropologist, explains that East Indians in Trinidad have 'managed to preserve much of their culture, if not intact at least in a functional and recognisable condition.' In his view, the 'fete' is the keystone and focus of Trinidadian culture. Crowley notes now the 'fetes' of Blacks and East Indians 'provide an invaluable meeting ground of common interest and understanding among all Trinidadians.' He then provides detailed descriptions of East Indian Hindu and Muslim festivals celebrated in Trinidad: the Ramleela in October, Divali in early November, and Hosse in the autumn.

Carnival

246 **Carnival à la Trinidad and Tobago.**
Clement B. G. London. *Americas*, vol. 29, no. 2 (Feb. 1977), p. 19-24. bibliog.

On the Monday and Tuesday before Ash Wednesday, Carnival takes place in Trinidad and Tobago, as it also does in New Orleans and in Brazil. London discusses the uniquely Trinidadian aspects of the festival from a variety of perspectives: historical, anthropological, psychological, and socio-cultural. He notes how the festival has changed since its inception in the 18th century, with the African element becoming more and more prominent. The article is nicely illustrated with black and white and colour photographs of the celebration.

247 **The Trinidad carnival; mandate for a national theatre.**
Errol Hill. Austin, Texas: University of Texas Press, 1972. 139p.

Norman Lederer, reviewing this book in the *Journal of American Folklore* [vol. 88, no. 348 (April-June 1975), p. 193-94] comments that 'Errol Hill, a professor of drama at Dartmouth and a native Trinidadian, provides an excellent overview of the origins and evolution of the myriad aspects of the carnival to support his thesis that the celebration contains the seeds of a national theatre.' The theatrical aspects of the Carnival – the calypso dramas, the masquerades, and the stage spectacles – are emphasized in the volume.

248 **Carnival in Trinidad.**
Howard LaFay, photographs by Winfield Parks. *National Geographic*, vol. 140, no. 5 (Nov. 1971), p. 693-701.

Brief text accompanies full-colour photographs of Trinidadians 'playing mas' (wearing costumes) and 'jumping up' (dancing) at Carnival time.

249 **Carnival in nineteenth century Trinidad.**
Andrew Pearse. *Caribbean Quarterly*, vol. 4, nos. 3-4 (March-June 1956), p. 175-93.

This excellent article, based on research in Trinidadian newspapers, is a history of Trinidad's Carnival from 1783 to 1900. Pearse discusses the form and content of the institution of Carnival in Trinidad, from the point of view of the changing culture and social structure of the island. It is in three sections: 'Pre-emancipation society and its Carnival'; 'Post-emancipation Carnival'; and 'Jamette Carnival.'

250 **The changing attitude of the coloured middle class toward Carnival.**
Barbara E. Powrie. *Caribbean Quarterly*, vol. 4, nos 3-4 (March-June 1956), p. 224-34.

An interesting adjunct to the literature on the Carnival itself. Powrie discusses the origins of Trinidad's coloured middle class and the social tensions to which it is subject. She sees the group as organized around the key concept of 'respectability,' and following a 'white' ideal of behaviour. In her view, the Carnival used to be the only social excitement formerly available within the coloured middle class's restrained existence: Carnival enabled members of this class to enjoy a brief period of freedom. At the time of writing, however, she believes that the coloured middle class has become bored with Carnival and feels a need for a new means of self-expression.

251 **The Dragon Band or Devil Band.**
Bruce Procope. *Caribbean Quarterly*, vol. 4, nos. 3-4 (March-June 1956), p. 275-80.

Detailed information on the Dragon Band or Devil Band that participates in the Trinidad Carnival. Procope traces its history from 1906, and goes on to describe its current membership, costumes, and performances.

252 **The Midnight Robbers.**
Daniel J. Crowley. *Caribbean Quarterly*, vol. 4, nos. 3-4 (March-June 1956), p. 263-74.

A study of the Carnival phenomenon of the 'Midnight Robber,' a disguised participant who accosts Carnival spectators. Crowley describes the costumes and transcribes the monologues of 'robbers' who appeared during the 1954 Carnival in Port-of-Spain and environs.

253 **Pierrot Grenade.**
Andrew T. Carr. *Caribbean Quarterly*, vol. 4, nos. 3-4 (March-June 1956), p. 281-314.

'Pierrot Grenade' is 'the supreme jester in the Trinidad Carnival.' Carr describes the masquerade adopted by those who impersonate this character covering costume, habits, performance and language. The article includes a transcription in patois or French Creole and its translation into English of a typical exchange between two seasoned 'Pierrot Grenade' masqueraders.

254 **The traditional masques of Carnival.**
Daniel J. Crowley. *Caribbean Quarterly*, vol. 4, nos. 3-4 (March-June 1956), p. 194-223.

A meticulously detailed study of the costumed bands that form the basic unit of Trinidad's Carnival. Illustrated with line drawings.

Religion

Afro-Caribbean cults

255 **Marchin' the pilgrims home: leadership and decision making in an Afro-Caribbean faith.**

Stephen D. Glazier. Westport, Connecticut: Greenwood Press, 1983. 165p. bibliog. (Contributions to the Study of Religions Series, no. 10).

An ethnography and analysis of the Spiritual Baptists of Trinidad, based on field data gathered by the author between 1976 and 1982. The volume attempts a fresh examination of the church – its rituals, leaders, membership, and beliefs – and seeks to correct misinterpretations by focusing on the faith's central values, as opposed to marginal aspects. 'Glazier finds that African retentions are not a central characteristic of Spiritual Baptists . . . the churches [are] subject to more dominant concerns about survival in a modern capitalist economy.' The major emphasis of the study is on the church as an institution.

256 **Religious cults of the Caribbean: Trinidad, Jamaica and Haiti.**

George Eaton Simpson. Rio Piedras, Puerto Rico: Institute of Caribbean Studies, University of Puerto Rico, 1980. 3rd enlarged ed. 347p. bibliog. (Caribbean Monograph Series, no. 15).

This book was first published in 1965 as *The Shango Cult in Trinidad.* In 1970, enlarged with material on Jamaica and Haiti, it appeared in a revised edition under its present title. The 1980 edition has been further augmented with material on religion in St. Lucia and a summary article 'Afro-American religions and religious behavior.' Simpson is the foremost authority on the study of Afro-American religions in the Caribbean, and his one-hundred-page essay 'Shango Cult in Trinidad' included in this volume, constitutes a mini-encyclopaedia on the practices, rituals, beliefs, and personae of the Shango Cult as Simpson studied it in 1960. Three other articles on Trinidadian Afro-American religion are included in the volume: 'The Shango Cult in Nigeria and in Trinidad,' 'Selected Yoruba rituals: 1964,' and 'The Shouters Church.' Photographs of Shango altars, shrines, and rital objects and of Spiritual Baptist altars and baptismal ceremonies accompany the text.

257 **Trance induction and hallucination in Spiritualist Baptist mourning.**
Colleen Ward, M. H. Beaubrun. *Journal of Psychological Anthropology*, vol. 2, no. 4 (Fall 1979), p. 479-88. bibliog.

The authors study trance and hallucinatory behaviour in Trinidad's Spiritual Baptist Church as it occurs within the context of ritual healing and mourning ceremonies.

258 **Black religions in the New World.**
George Eaton Simpson. New York: Columbia University Press, 1978. 415p. maps. bibliog.

An authoritative study of Afro-American New World religions that includes the Black religious experience in Trinidad and Tobago – in the historically Christian churches, in neo-African Shango and in the revivalist Spiritual Baptist ('Shouters') Church. Simpson compares Shango and 'Shouters' in Trinidad, and also contrasts the Trinidadian version of Shango with the cult as it exists on the neighbouring island of Grenada.

259 **Yoruba religion in Trinidad: transfer and reinterpretation.**
Maureen Warner Lewis. *Caribbean Quarterly*, vol. 24, no. 3-4 (Sept.-Dec. 1978), p. 18-32.

A reviewer in the *Handbook of Latin American Studies* comments that in this article, Warner 'relates the world-view of a third-generation Yoruba descendant in Trinidad. Information obtained through interviews. Original piece of work.'

260 **Afro-American religions and religious behavior.**
George Eaton Simpson. *Caribbean Studies*, vol. 12, no. 2 (July 1972), p. 5-30. bibliog.

Compares the less orthodox New World Afro-American religious groups in their beliefs and behaviours. Trinidad Shango is included. Comparisons are made between the acculturative processes, the psychological aspects, and the political implications of the cults. Deities, soul concepts, shrines and temples, ritual objects and ceremonial practices are described and contrasted.

261 **Ritual dissociation and possession in Caribbean Negro religion.**
Erica Bourguignon. In: *Afro-American anthropology; contemporary perspectives*. Edited by Norman E. Whitten, John F. Szwed. New York: Free Press; London: Collier-Macmillan, 1970, p. 87-101.

Summarizes possession practices and beliefs common among the black masses of the Caribbean region. Bourguignon examines two types of religious groupings among black lower class populations in which possession experiences are valued: Afro-American, Afro-Catholic spirit cults and independent, fundamentalist Pentecostal churches. Both types of religious groupings are represented in Trinidad: the former by the Shango Cult and the latter by the Spiritual Baptists or 'Shouters.' Although Bourguignon takes her principal examples of these religious types from Haitian Voodoo and the Spiritual Baptists ('Shakers') of St. Vincent, Trinidadian varieties are referred to for contrast and comparison.

262 **Shango-Kult und Shouter-Kirche auf Trinidad und Grenada.**
(Shango Cult and Shouter Church in Trinidad and Grenada.)
Angelina Pollak-Eltz. *Anthropos*, vol. 65, no. 5-6 (1970), p. 814-32. bibliog.

A synthesis of published information on the two Afro-Caribbean faiths, the Shango Cult and the Spiritual Baptist ('Shouters') Church. In German.

263 **The Yoruba ancestor cult in Gasparillo; its structure, organization, and social function in community life.**
J. D. Elder. *Caribbean Quarterly*, vol. 16, no. 3 (Sept. 1970), p. 5-20.

Provides information on a Yoruba ancestor-worship cult in Gasparillo, Trinidad. Elder compares Trinidadian ceremonial practices with Yoruba ritual in Nigeria.

264 **Baptismal 'Mourning' and 'Building' ceremonies of the Shouters in Trinidad.**
George Eaton Simpson. *Journal of American Folklore*, vol. 79, no. 314 (Oct.-Dec. 1966), p. 537-50.

A study of ceremonies performed by the 'Shouters' or Spiritual Baptists, a black charismatic fundamentalist sect that flourishes in Trinidad. Simpson meticulously describes the ceremonies as he observed them in 1960. Some interesting illustrations of 'spiritual' writing, a phenomenon practiced by members of the sect, accompany the text. The article is reprinted in *Religious cults of the Caribbean: Trinidad, Jamaica and Haiti* (q.v.).

265 **Social stratification in an Afro-American cult.**
Frances Henry. *Anthropological Quarterly*, vol. 38, no. 2 (April 1965), p. 72-78. bibliog.

This article discusses how status is acquired by cult members within an Afro-American cult and what the effects of having a high or a low status in the cult are. Henry notes that spirit possession is one of the major means by which status is acquired and lists the aspects of possession that determine or enhance status. She identifies three levels of cultic sub-grouping: the high status power clique of leaders, the intermediate status group, and the low status group. Most cult members fall into the intermediate group consisting of those who have some status but are always striving to increase it. Based on fieldwork conducted in 1956, 1958, and 1959.

266 **Selected Yoruba rituals: 1964.**
George Eaton Simpson. *Nigerian Journal of Economic and Social Studies*, vol. 7, no. 3 (Nov. 1965), p. 311-24.

These detailed descriptions of six annual ceremonies of the traditional Yoruba religion, based on fieldwork in Nigeria are of interest to Trinidadists because of the link between Trinidad's Shango Cult and the religion of the Yoruba. Reprinted in *Religious cults of the Caribbean: Trinidad, Jamaica and Haiti* (q.v.).

267 **The acculturative process in Trinidadian Shango.**
George Eaton Simpson. *Anthropological Quarterly*, vol. 37, no. 1 (Jan. 1964), p. 16-27. bibliog.

In this study conducted in 1966, Simpson first describes the belief system, ritual paraphernalia, and ceremonies of Trinidad's Shango Cult. He then discusses the acculturative process in the religion, categorizing Shango elements in four categories: full or nearly full African retentions; reinterpretations of African elements; syncretisms; and European-borrowed traits and reinterpretations of European elements. Simpson concludes by considering recent changes in Trinidadian Shango and what these may portend for its future, particularly the 'mixing' of Shango and Spiritual Baptist beliefs and rituals.

268 **The Shango cult in Nigeria and in Trinidad.**
George Eaton Simpson. *American Anthropologist*, vol. 64, no. 6 (Dec. 1962), p. 1,204-19. bibliog.

Simpson notes that 'a comparison of the Shango cults of the Yoruba of southwestern Nigeria and of lower class people of African descent in Trinidad reveals interesting similarities and differences in the form and meaning of a number of culture elements.' This article contrasts and discusses the deities, temples, ritual objects, divination, ceremonial practices, soul concepts, witches, healing, dreams, charms, social organization, cult centres, and cultists of the two countries. The article also includes a section on the acculturation process as it occurs in Trinidadian Shango. Reprinted in *Religious cults of the Caribbean: Trinidad, Jamaica and Haiti* (q.v.).

269 **Psychological aspects of spirit possession.**
Walter Mischel, Frances Mischel. *American Anthropologist*, vol. 60, no. 2, part 1 (April 1958), p. 249-60. bibliog.

The Mischels offer a detailed description of spirit possession behaviour as they observed it among Trinidad's Shango cultists in the summer of 1956. They report on the induction of the possession trance, the various levels of intensity achieved during the experience, and recovery from the possession trance. The Mischels then analyse spirit possession behaviour from a psychological point of view, hypothesizing 'that the practice of spirit possession permits the sanctioned expression of behaviors which are otherwise socially unacceptable or unavailable.'

270 **'African powers' in Trinidad: the Shango Cult.**
Frances Mischel. *Anthropological Quarterly*, vol. 30, no. 2 (April 1957), p. 45-59.

Based on research conducted in Trinidad in the summer of 1956, Mischel provides a mini-reference work on the Shango gods. Her article covers the Shango deities and ritual activities, providing detailed descriptions of the 'feasts' or 'sacrifices' – the main ceremonies that take place in the Shango religion – and of the Shango cosmology of 'heavenly powers.' The article ends with a list of these 'powers', which are the major deities of the cult, with their characteristics, implements, days, sacrifices, sacred colours, and counterparts among the Christian saints.

271 **My life.**
Frank Mayhew. *Caribbean Quarterly*, vol. 3, no. 1 (1953), p. 13-23.

This autobiography of the pastor of a Spiritual Baptist or 'Shouters' Church in Trinidad constitutes a mystical odyssey.

272 **A Rada community in Trinidad.**
Andrew T. Carr. *Caribbean Quarterly*, vol. 3, no. 1 (1953), p. 35-54.

A descriptive, anthropological study of the Trinidadian religious community of Belmont, founded by immigrants from Dahomey in 1868. Carr describes the Rada group as it existed in the 1950s. Cultic practices and beliefs are detailed; and the Rada pantheon, or the Big People, are listed along with their colours, symbols, and Christian counterparts. Rada ceremonies, including the central sacrificial ceremony called a Voduna or Saraka, and music and dancing are described. Carr remarks that the Belmont community has succeeded in preserving African beliefs and customs. Photographs by Eugene Beard.

Music

273 **Spiritual Baptist music of Trinidad.**
New York: Folkways Record and Service Corporation, 1980. [Phonodisc]. (Folkways FE4234).

The music of the Spiritual Baptist Cult, recorded in Trinidad by Stephen D. Glazier.

274 **Cult music of Trinidad.**
New York: Folkways Records and Service Corporation, 1961. [Phonodisc]. (Folkways Ethnic Library Album FE4478).

Music of the Shango Cult, recorded in Trinidad by George Eaton Simpson. Includes a four-page booklet of programme notes by Simpson.

Christianity

275 **Presbyterian missions to Trinidad and Puerto Rico.**
Graeme S. Mount. Hantsport, Nova Scotia, Canada: Lancelet Press, 1983. 356p. maps. bibliog.

Concerns the Canadian Presbyterian Mission to Trinidad during the years 1868 to 1914.

276 **Missionary methods and local responses: the Canadian Presbyterians and the East Indians in the Caribbean.**
Brinsley Samaroo. In: *East Indians in the Caribbean; colonialism and the struggle for identity: papers presented to a symposium on East Indians in the Caribbean, the University of the West Indies, June 1975.* Preface by Bridget Brereton, Winston Dookeran, with an introduction by V. S. Naipaul. Millwood, New York, London; Nendeln, Liechtenstein: Kraus International, 1982, p. 93-115.

An extremely interesting history and discussion of attempts by Presbyterian missionaries, from 1868 to the present, to win converts among the East Indians in Trinidad and Guyana. The predominantly Scottish/Canadian Maritime Presbyterian Mission was started in the Caribbean by the Presbyterian Church of Nova Scotia in 1868, with Trinidad as its base. The missionaries were aggressive in their pursuit of converts, and were encouraged by the government in this aim, but the hoped-for mass conversions did not take place: today Presbyterians form only six per cent of Trinidad's population and few missionaries remain.

277 **Catholic Church in Trinidad, 1797-1820.**
Vincent Leahy. Arima, Trinidad and Tobago: St. Dominic Press, 1980. 218p. (West Indian Church History, 1).

A history of the Roman Catholic Church during the earliest period of British colonialism in Trinidad.

278 **Perspectives on Pentecostalism: case studies from the Caribbean and Latin America.**
Edited by Stephen D. Glazier. Washington, DC: University Press of America, 1980. 197p.

Includes Stephen Glazier's essay 'Pentecostal exorcism and modernization in Trinidad,' (p. 67-80) in which he describes a Pentecostal service that includes exorcism. Glazier sees the Pentecostal Church as a modernizing influence because of the values espoused from the pulpit by its pastors.

279 **Mission and leadership among the 'Meriken' Baptists of Trinidad.**
John O. Stewart. In: *LAAG contributions to Afro-American ethnohistory in Latin America and the Caribbean.* Compiled by Norman E. Whitten, Jr. Washington, DC: Latin American Anthropology Group, American Anthropological Association, 1976, p. 17-25. bibliog. (Contributions of the Latin American Anthropology Group, no. 1).

In this paper, originally presented at a 1976 symposium, Stewart describes American black Baptists who migrated to Trinidad.

280 **The Presbyterian Canadian Mission as an agent of integration in Trinidad during the nineteenth and early twentieth centuries.**
Brinsley Samaroo. *Caribbean Studies*, vol. 14, no. 4 (Jan. 1975), p. 41-55.

Emphasizes the role played by Canadian Protestant missionaries in facilitating the East Indians' adaptation to a totally unfamiliar society in Trinidad in the years 1870 to 1920.

281 **Anglican problems of adaptation in the Catholic Caribbean – the C.M.S. in Trinidad 1836-1844.**
J. E. Pinnington. *Journal of Caribbean History*, vol. 1 (Nov. 1970), p. 23-40.

The Church Missionary Society (CMS) provided evangelical mission clergy to the Caribbean area. In this article, Pinnington discusses the Church of England's relations with these non-Anglican Protestant clergy and with the Roman Catholic Church in post-emancipation Trinidad.

282 **My missionary memories.**
Kenneth James Grant. Halifax, Nova Scotia, Canada: The Imperial Publishing Company, 1923. 203p.

Grant was involved with missionary work among the East Indians in the West Indies. In this book, he tells the story of the Trinidad Presbyterian Mission up to 1907.

283 **John Morton of Trinidad; pioneer missionary of the Presbyterian Church in Canada to the East Indians in the British West Indies: journals, letters and papers.**
John Morton, edited by Sarah E. Morton. Toronto: Westminster Company, 1916. 491p. maps.

Presbyterian clergyman John Morton spent forty years working for the conversion to Christianity of Trinidad's East Indians.

Hinduism

284 **The Hindu sacraments (*rites de passage*) in Trinidad and Tobago.**
J. C. Jha. *Caribbean Quarterly*, vol. 22, no. 1 (March 1976), p. 40-52.

Jha explains the sixteen main sacraments or rituals which celebrate the Hindu life-cycle, giving the most detailed treatment to the Hindu marriage ceremony. Jha describes how the performance of Hindu rituals has been abbreviated among the East Indians of Trinidad, where emphasis has shifted from the religious to the social aspects of the sacraments.

285 **Differential socio-religious adaptation.**
Barton M. Schwartz. *Social and Economic Studies*, vol. 16, no. 3 (Sept. 1967), p. 237-48.

A study of the forms taken by Hinduism among the East Indians of Trinidad. Schwartz focuses his study on the Sanatan Dharma Maha Sabha sect in a single village called 'Boodram', whose lay population evinces a selective attitude towards and a selective acceptance of the Hindu religion.

286 **Extra-legal activities of the village pandit in Trinidad.**
Barton M. Schwartz. *Anthropological Quarterly*, vol. 38, no. 2 (April 1965), p. 62-71. bibliog.

Based on fieldwork undertaken in 1961 in the southwestern Trinidad village of 'Boodram', whose 850 inhabitants are 97% East Indian. Schwartz discusses the role of the village pandit, a Hindu religious specialist, in arbitrating disputes between village families or individuals. The article includes an example of a case that was settled by a pandit. Schwartz ends with a discussion of the social control function of the pandit among Trinidad's East Indian population.

287 **Ritual aspects of caste in Trinidad.**
Barton M. Schwartz. *Anthropological Quarterly*, vol. 37, no. 1 (Jan. 1964), p. 1-15.

Schwartz finds that rituals expressing caste have been modified and that theology is for the most part ignored among the Hindus of Trinidad.

Society and Culture

General

288 **Indian heritage in Trinidad (West Indies).**

J. C. Jha. *Eastern Anthropologist*, vol. 27, no. 3 (July-Sept. 1974), p. 211-34. bibliog.

Jha compares Hindu and Muslim customs and traditions as they are practised on the Indian subcontinent with their current status in Trinidad. He is able to point out many survivals and adaptations of such traditions, which leads him to conclude that the 'Indian heritage in Trinidad seems to have been largely retained and some of the facets of Indian culture which had been swept away by the flood of westernization or modernization are being revived.' The article is informative with regard to the details of Indian religious and cultural practices.

289 **West Indian societies.**

David Lowenthal. New York: Oxford University Press, 1972. 385p. map. bibliog. (American Geographical Society Research Series, no. 26).

A richly informative volume on the non-Hispanic societies of the West Indies. Lowenthal tells who the West Indians are and, emphasizing the importance of race and colour, describes how their society is organized in respect both to itself and to the outside world. Includes chapters on history, social structure, East Indians and Creoles, ethnic minorities, emigration and neo-colonialism, and racial and national identity. The volume contains an excellent bibliography.

290 **History, ecology, and demography in the British Caribbean: an analysis of East Indian ethnicity.**
Allen S. Ehrlich. *Southwestern Journal of Anthropology*, vol. 27, no. 2 (Summer 1971), p. 166-80. maps. bibliog.

An inquiry into why East Indian cultural patterns did not persist among East Indian immigrants to Jamaica, as they did in Trinidad and Guyana. Ehrlich compares the three countries with regard to the level of development of the plantation system; the natural environment; and the adaptational patterns of the emancipated slaves. The ways that these three factors interacted in the three countries were quite distinct, and thus affected the concentration or dispersal of East Indian indentured labourers. This, in turn, was crucial with regard to the retention or loss of East Indian culture.

291 **Peoples and cultures of the Caribbean; an anthropological reader.**
Edited and with an introduction by Michael M. Horowitz. Garden City, New York: Natural History Press, 1971. 606p. map. bibliog.

Horowitz's introduction discusses the anthropological orientations used in the study of the Caribbean region. The body of the book consists of reprinted articles on individual countries. Two essays deal directly with Trinidad: Andrew Pearse's 'Carnival in nineteenth century Trinidad,' p. 528-52, reprinted from *Caribbean Quarterly* (q.v.) and Morton Klass's 'Life cycle in an East Indian village in Trinidad,' p. 436-47, reprinted from his *East Indians in Trinidad: a study of cultural persistence* (q.v.). Trinidad also serves as the primary example in Lloyd F. Braithwaite's 'Social stratification and cultural pluralism,' p. 95-116, reprinted from the *Annals of the New York Academy of Sciences*.

292 **Some preliminary observations on the Chinese in Trinidad.**
Gerald Bentley, Frances Henry. In: *McGill studies in Caribbean anthropology.* Edited by Frances Henry. Montreal: Centre for Developing Area Studies, McGill University, 1969, p. 19-33. (McGill University, Montreal. Centre for Developing Area Studies. Occasional Paper Series, no. 5).

Based on a field investigation in Trinidad in 1967, this study finds that the island's Chinese have become Creolized and Westernized.

293 **The natural experiment, ecology and culture.**
Morris Freilich. *Southwestern Journal of Anthropology*, vol. 19, no. 1 (Spring 1963), p. 21-39.

Freilich explains the natural experiment 'as one where the researcher selects a situation for study where change of a clear and dramatic nature has occurred.' Freilich found the necessary conditions for a natural experiment in the Trinidadian village of Anamat, where he was able to observe Black Creole and East Indian peasants while using ecological variables as controls. The article is of most interest for its contrast of the East Indian and Black cultural value systems which Freilich found operating in the village.

294 **East Indians in Trinidad: a study of cultural persistence.**
Morton Klass. New York: Columbia University Press, 1961. 265p. map. bibliog.

This work of cultural anthropology is an example of the community study method applied to a civilization transported to a foreign environment. Klass studied the East Indian community in a Trinidadian village called Amity in 1957-1958. It is his contention that the East Indian immigrants who founded Amity were able to reconstitute a community reflecting their society of origin. He feels that kinship, caste, praja relationships, and the Indian life-cycle have persisted, as has Hinduism, among the East Indians of Trinidad. The book covers the physical setting, work, marriage and family, religion, and community organization of the village.

295 **East Indians in the West Indies.**
Arthur Niehoff, Juanita Niehoff. Milwaukee, Wisconsin: Milwaukee Public Museum, 1960. 192p. map. bibliog. (Milwaukee Public Museum. Publication in Anthropology, no. 6).

An anthropological study providing an introduction to the East Indians and their culture in Trinidad.

296 **The East Indians in Trinidad; a study of an immigrant community.**
M. B. Naidoo. *Journal of Geography*, vol. 59, no. 4 (April 1960), p. 175-81. maps.

This article, which is suitable for secondary school or new undergraduate students, provides a sketch of the East Indians of Trinidad as Naidoo observed them in the spring of 1959. Naidoo sees the Trinidadian East Indians as clinging to their Hindu and Indian culture and customs.

297 **Trinidad village.**
Melville J. Herskovits, Frances S. Herskovits. New York: Knopf, 1947. Reprinted, New York: Octagon Books, 1964. 351p. bibliog.

A pioneering work by an eminent American cultural anthropologist. Herskovits sought the African elements in black Trinidadian culture, using the concepts of cultural retention, cultural focus, and cultural reinterpretation to organize his work. He and his wife studied the Blacks in Toco, northeastern Trinidad, in 1939. Their book covers work, domestic life, the family, mating, rites, religion, divination, and magic among the inhabitants of the village. The volume includes an interesting chapter on the 'Shouters' sect in Toco. An appendix contains 'Notes on Shango worship' and 'Official documents prohibiting Shouters practices and Obeah.'

Social class and social change

298 **Class formation and class and race relations in the West Indies.**
Cecilia A. Karch. In: *Middle classes in dependent countries.* Edited by Dale L. Johnson. Beverly Hills, California: Sage Publications, 1985, p. 107-36. bibliog. (Class, State, and Development, no. 3).

In this study of 'the dynamic between changing forms of international capitalism, the historical formation of classes, and contemporary class and race relations in the Commonwealth Caribbean' from the 19th century to the present, Trinidad, where the class, race, colour dynamic has been particularly acute, receive a good deal of attention.

299 **Social change and the East Indians in rural Trinidad; a critique of methodologies.**
Joseph Nevadomsky. *Social and Economic Studies*, vol. 31, no. 1 (March 1982), p. 90-126. bibliog.

An excellent summary of sociological and anthropological work on the East Indians of Trinidad. Nevadomsky reviews and criticises the models that have been used to organize the study of persistence and change in East Indian culture: the systematic model, the plural society model, and the retentionist model. The bibliography lists sixty-nine books, periodical articles, and papers dealing with the East Indians in the Caribbean area.

300 **Street life; Afro-American culture in urban Trinidad.**
Michael Lieber. Boston, Massachusetts: G. K. Hall; Cambridge, Massachusetts: Schenkman Publishing, 1981. 118p. bibliog.

A careful ethnographic description of the lifestyles of a group of lower-class Black men in Port-of-Spain. The study is based on fieldwork conducted in 1969 and 1970-1971. Of special interest are a detailed description of the neighbourhoods of Port-of-Spain (p. 20-29), and information on Trinidad's marijuana trade (p. 72-81).

301 **Race, social class and the origins of the occupational elite in Trinidad and Tobago.**
Farley S. Brathwaite. *Boletin de Estudios Latinoamericanos*, vol. 28 (June 1980), p. 13-29.

Five Trinidadian élite occupational groups – doctors, lawyers, accountants, secondary school teachers, and nurses – were surveyed to obtain data on the role played by race and class factors in their origins. Brathwaite's analysis of the data reveals that social class is more influential than race, but that other factors are also important.

302 **Stereotypes of Negroes and East Indians in Trinidad: a re-examination.**
Ishmael J. Baksh. *Caribbean Quarterly*, vol. 25, nos. 1-2 (March-June 1979), p. 52-71.

Baksh challenges the stereotypes of lower-class Blacks and East Indians in Trinidad. From a study of the results of a questionnaire administered to fifth-form public secondary school students in 1972, he concludes that changes in Trinidad's social structure have resulted in favourable perceptions of the accessibility of the more prestigious jobs on the part of both Black and East Indian students.

303 **Caribbean social relations.**
Edited by Colin G. Clarke. Liverpool, England: Centre for Latin American Studies, University of Liverpool, 1978. 95p. maps. bibliog. (University of Liverpool. Centre for Latin American Studies. Monograph Series, no. 8).

This collection of scholarly papers presented at a symposium held at the University of Liverpool in May, 1975, includes Stephanie Goodenough's 'Race, status and urban ecology in Port of Spain, Trinidad,' in which she finds that the primary determinant of class and place of residence in that city is race.

304 **Pluralism, race and class in Caribbean society.**
Stuart Hall. In: *Race and class in post-colonial society: a study of ethnic group relations in the English-speaking Caribbean, Bolivia, Chile and Mexico*. Paris: UNESCO, 1977, p. 150-82. bibliog.

In this general discussion of the Anglophone former British colonies, Hall argues that in the British colonial post-emancipation stage, these societies moved from a caste (pre-emancipation) system to a class structure, and in their present post-independence or decolonizing stage, ethnic segments have become important. 'The work required to describe this "decolonizing" national society . . . remains to be done.'

305 **Upward mobility and career (value) orientation: an empirical test of the embourgeoisement thesis.**
Farley S. Braithwaite. *Caribbean Studies*, vol. 16, no. 3-4 (Oct. 1976-Jan. 1977), p. 149-69.

The project reported in this article, which was part of a larger survey on secondary school teachers in Trinidad and Tobago, seeks 'to make some contribution to the embourgeoisement debate by providing some data on occupational mobility and career orientation in Trinidad and Tobago society.' Three value areas: career aspirations, career expectations, and occupational values, are examined to see if the nature and extent to which there are differences in these areas between the different social classes in Trinidad and Tobago can be identified.

306 **The East Indian middle class today.**
John Gaffar La Guerre. In: *Calcutta to Caroni: the East Indians of Trinidad.* Edited by John Gaffar La Guerre. Port-of-Spain: Longmans Caribbean, 1974, p. 98-107.

An examination of the problems facing East Indians in finding their place in post-independence Trinidad.

307 **Stratification and political change in Trinidad and Jamaica.**
Carl Stone. Beverly Hills, California: Sage, 1974. 39p. bibliog. (Sage Professional Papers in Comparative Politics, Series no. 01-026).

A Jamaican political sociologist considers political change in relation to social class in his country and in Trinidad.

308 **Social mobility and secondary school selection in Trinidad and Tobago.**
Malcolm Cross, Allan M. Schwartzbaum. *Social and Economic Studies*, vol. 18, no. 2 (June 1969), p. 189-207.

This research study examines several variables in order to determine to what extent they can be correlated with the choice of secondary school. The authors find that socio-economic factors are the most significant predictors.

309 **Caste in overseas Indian communities.**
Edited by Barton M. Schwartz. San Francisco: Chandler, 1967. 350p. map. bibliog. (Chandler Publications in Anthropology and Sociology).

The basic question that united these essays: does caste exist in overseas Indian communities? receives a definite 'no' with regard to Trinidad from scholars who have studied the institution there. Barton M. Schwartz in 'The failure of caste in Trinidad' (p. 117-47) points out the disappearance of caste in a Trinidad village. Arthur Niehoff in 'The function of caste among the Indians of the Oropuche Lagoon, Trinidad' (p. 149-63) finds little observance of caste occupation or rules of ritual cleanliness among the inhabitants of two rural towns. Colin Clarke in 'Caste among Hindus in a town in Trinidad: San Fernando' (p. 165-99) claims that the caste system has broken down in Trinidad, although some feeling about it persists.

310 **Race and color in the West Indies.**
David Lowenthal. *Daedalus*, vol. 96, no. 2 (Spring 1967), p. 580-626. bibliog.

A readable presentation of the social intricacies associated with race and colour in the Caribbean area, with Trinidad mentioned in context. 'Nowhere in the West Indies does racial discrimination have the sanction of law, and social exclusion based on color, once the rule, is now much moderated. But color distinctions correlate with class differences and govern most personal associations.'

311 **The development of the middle class in the Caribbean.**
P. M. Sherlock. In: *The development of a middle class in tropical and sub-tropical areas.* Brussels: International Institute of Differing Civilizations, 1956, p. 324-30. bibliog.

A general presentation of the political, economic, and social aspects of the British Caribbean middle class of the colonial era. 'The West Indian middle class of today [i.e. 1956] is made up largely of coloured people of Afro-European origins'; it also included some Blacks, East Indians, Chinese, Syrians, and Europeans.

312 **Social stratification in Trinidad; a preliminary analysis.**
Lloyd Braithwaite. *Social and Economic Studies*, vol. 2, nos. 2-3 (Oct. 1953), p. 5-175. bibliog. Reprinted, Mona, Jamaica: Institute of Social and Economic Research, University of the West Indies, 1975. 170p. bibliog.

One of the first studies on this subject, Braithwaite's work covers in detail the various systems of social stratification based on race, class, and colour operating within Trinidadian society when the island was a British colony. The study is based on field-work conducted between 1950 and 1952. Braithwaite does not include an analysis of the social position occupied by Trinidad's East Indians.

Values

313 **Self and society: attitudes of students in India, Iran, Trinidad-Tobago and the United States.**
Edwin D. Driver. *Sociological Bulletin*, vol. 30, no. 2 (Sept. 1981), p. 118-36. bibliog.

A reprint of lectures delivered at the University of Massachusetts, Amherst, in April, 1981. Between 1974 and 1980 Driver administered the 'Twenty Statement Test' to undergraduate students in the four countries mentioned in the title. He examines the four nations with regard to their profiles of the self, his aim being to find the mixture of positive and negative elements, the difference between male and female perceptions of the self, and the effect of educational instruction on the self. He then compares and contrasts his findings for the four groups.

314 **Perceptual style, locus of control and personality variables among East Indians and Blacks in Trinidad.**
I. W. Stuart, D. Murgatroyd, L. Denmark. *International Journal of Social Psychiatry*, vol. 24, no. 1 (Spring 1978), p. 26-32.

The authors compare personality and psychological factors of the two main ethnic groups in Trinidad.

315 **Political socialisation among adolescents in school – a comparative study of Barbados, Guyana and Trinidad.**
W. W. Anderson, R. W. Grant. *Social and Economic Studies*, vol. 26, no. 2 (June 1977), p. 217-33. bibliog.

An attempt 'to examine the "state of affairs" in the crucial area of political learning . . . a preliminary analysis of several contingent areas without any attempt at grand theory.' Empirical data were drawn from the secondary school population in Barbados, Guyana, and Trinidad. Approximately two hundred Trinidadian students answered a questionnaire designed to show what they know and how they feel about social changes.

316 **Understanding calypso content: a critique and an alternative explanation.**
Roy L. Austin. *Caribbean Quarterly*, vol. 22, nos. 2-3 (June-Sept. 1976), p. 74-83. bibliog.

Austin's reply to J. D. Elder's 'The male/female conflict in calypso' (q.v.), provides an alternate explanation for Elder's data, and is itself an interesting discussion of the female's role in Trinidadian society.

317 **The debate on the structure and content of West Indian values: some relevant data from Trinidad and Tobago.**
Patricia Madoo Lengermann. *British Journal of Sociology*, vol. 23, no. 3 (Sept. 1972), p. 298-311.

Lengermann reviews four competing sociological theses that provide interpretations of West Indian culture: cultural pluralism, cultural consensus, cultural variation, and increasing modernism. Using each of these theses, she analyses attitudinal data collected in 1967 through interviews with 268 male Trinidadians in order to determine whether their value orientations can be classified as traditional or modern.

318 **Working-class values in Trinidad and Tobago.**
Patricia Madoo Lengermann. *Social and Economic Studies*, vol. 20, no. 2 (June 1971), p. 151-63.

The result of a research project carried out in 1967, this paper describes 'a certain set of working-class value orientations in Trinidad, in terms of their relative modernity.' Lengermann bases her findings on an analysis of replies made to a structured, hour-long questionnaire administered to 240 male Trinidadians.

319 **Secondary school environment and development: the case of Trinidad and Tobago.**
Allen M. Schwartzbaum, Malcolm Cross. *Social and Economic Studies*, vol. 19, no. 3 (Sept. 1970), p. 368-88.

A sociological research study conducted in Trinidad and Tobago. 'The object of this paper is to examine the relationship between school environment and student values in a developing nation. The paper investigates the extent to which the average social-economic composition of the school affects students' mobility orientation.'

320 **Socio-political perceptions and attitudes of East Indian elites in Trinidad.**
Yogendra K. Malik. *Western Political Quarterly*, vol. 23, no. 3 (Sept. 1970), p. 552-63.

Based on interviews with eighty-nine East Indian leaders in 1965. 'The questions investigated in this study were who the East Indian leaders were and what their attitudes were toward various social, economic, and political issues. Answers to these questions give us insight into their value orientation, the extent of their participation in the pluralistic social structure, the depth of their ethnocentricity, and their evaluation of the existing political system.'

321 **Agencies of political socialization and East Indian ethnic identification in Trinidad.**
Yogendra K. Malik. *Sociological Bulletin*, vol. 18, no. 2 (Sept. 1969), p. 101-21. bibliog.

Malik discusses the sources – the home, Hindu organizations, and various religious sects – of the political values, standards, attitudes, and feelings of Trinidad's East Indian élite. He offers some interesting insights into the differing attitudes of East Indian Hindus, Muslims, and Christians towards such topics as inter-religious marriages and the caste system. Malik feels that Indian culture has survived in Trinidad.

322 **We wish to be looked upon: a study of the aspirations of youth in a developing society.**
Vera Rubin, Marisa Zavalloni. New York: Teachers College Press, 1969. 257p. bibliog.

Young Trinidadians speak for themselves in this study based on 'two successive surveys of the aspirations of youth which were undertaken in Trinidad and Tobago on the eve of major changes in the sociopolitical situation.' The first survey took place in 1957, the second in 1961. Nine hundred and sixty students took part, writing 'an autobiography of the future' and answering a questionnaire. Rubin and Zavalloni analyse these responses in order to determine the young people's perception of the world and their place in it.

323 **The male/female conflict in calypso.**
J. D. Elder. *Caribbean Quarterly*, vol. 14, no. 3 (Sept. 1968), p. 23-41.

Elder scrutinizes the folk-song tradition of Trinidad and Tobago through the lens of psychoanalytic concepts in order to explore 'the major characteristics of popular social mores and traditional culture patterns' in the islands, as they relate to the theme of male vs. female as expressed in calypsoes.

324 **Values of Negro and East Indian school children in Trinidad.**
Helen Bagenstose Green. *Social and Economic Studies*, vol. 14, no. 2 (June 1965), p. 204-16.

Green administered three questionnaires to Fourth Form classes in forty-one randomly selected Trinidad primary schools. The subjects were all from low-income families and their average age was 12.6 years. Black students outnumbered East Indians. According to her analysis of the data collected through this project, Green found that Black 'adolescents show a broad social orientation in contrast to the East Indians' more intensive concern for a few persons.' Black 'youngsters are more self-reliant, unpredictable, and expressive, whereas the East Indian group are more insecure, restrained and conscious of blame that should follow wrong-doing.'

325 **Socialization values in the Negro and East Indian sub-cultures of Trinidad.**
Helen Bagenstose Green. *Journal of Social Psychology*, vol. 64, first half (Oct. 1964), p. 1-26.

'This is a cross-cultural comparison of socialization values held by Negro and East Indian mothers in Trinidad . . . measured by an interview schedule on child-training intentions administered to maternity cases [in the free wards of the Colonial General Hospital, Port-of-Spain].' Green reviews the work done in this field, describes her research design and procedure, then discusses her findings. The hypothesis that was supported by the study was: 'Negro mothers were found to value extra-family involvement more than did East Indian mothers.' The Black mothers also valued autonomous independence and direct expression.

326 **The lower-class value stretch.**
Hyman Rodman. *Social Forces*, vol. 42, no. 2 (Dec. 1963), p. 205-15.

'The lower-class value stretch refers to the wider range of values, and the lower degree of commitment to these values, to be found within the lower class. Data on level of aspiration studies and on illegitimacy in the Caribbean are presented to support the idea that the value stretch is the major response to the lower class to its deprived situation.' Rodman presents data drawn from his field work in a Black, lower-class village in Trinidad in order to exemplify his 'value-stretch' thesis.

327 **Preference for delayed reinforcement and social responsibility.**
Walter Mischel. *Journal of Abnormal and Social Psychology*, vol. 62, no. 1 (Jan. 1961), p. 1-7. bibliog.

Trinidadian subjects, aged twelve to fourteen, were used in this study exploring the relationship between reward preference and social responsibility; delinquent behaviour; and accuracy in time standards.

328 **Delay of gratification, need for achievement, and acquiescence in another culture.**
Walter Mischel. *Journal of Abnormal Psychology*, vol. 62, no. 3 (May 1961), p. 543-52. bibliog.

A study carried out in a school in Trinidad and Tobago in which 112 Trinidadian Black children, aged eleven to fourteen, were tested on their choice behaviour with respect to reward preferences as related to the need for achievement and acquiescence.

329 **Father-absence and delay of gratification: cross-cultural comparisons.**
Walter Mischel. *Journal of Abnormal and Social Psychology*, vol. 63, no. 1 (July 1961), p. 116-24. bibliog.

A research study, based on investigations in Trinidad and Grenada. One aim of the study was to relate children's preferences for delayed gratification to the variable of the presence or absence of a father in the child's home. A second aim was to compare personality differences between Black groups in the two islands, and a third was to compare Black and East Indian groups in Trinidad in regard to their preferences for delayed vs. immediate gratification. Mischel describes his study, and goes on to discuss its results.

330 **Cultural models and land holdings.**
Morris Freilich. *Anthropological Quarterly*, vol. 23, no. 4 (Oct. 1960), p. 188-97. bibliog.

Freilich explains how he used 'prediction of the past' to verify a cultural model of the direction of land change among Blacks and East Indians in Trinidad where the first group has gradually lost land to the second. Freilich sums up East Indian vs. Creole cultural value systems in a handy table that compares the two groups with regard to their orientations about time, space, people (kinship units and associational patterns), authority, exchange (goods and services and women), sanctions, and goals. The article also includes a table of land holding change in Trinidad according to ethnic group.

331 **On understanding lower-class behavior.**
Hyman Rodman. *Social and Economic Studies*, vol. 8, no. 4 (Dec. 1959), p. 441-50. bibliog.

Rodman asks the question, 'To what extent do [a middle-class person's] middle class values lead him to misinterpret lower-class behaviour?' In his answer, he brings to bear insights gained from field work among lower class Black families in Trinidad.

332 **Preference for delayed reinforcement: an experimental study of a cultural observation.**

Walter Mischel. *Journal of Abnormal and Social Psychology*, vol. 56, no. 1 (Jan. 1958), p. 57-61. bibliog.

Mischel tested fifty-three Trinidadian male and female children, aged seven to nine, in 'an attempt to validate, experimentally, an observation about cultural differences formulated during the course of a "culture and personality" field research.' The observation was that, supposedly, 'when given a chance, the [Black] is said to be characterized by preference for relatively smaller, immediate reinforcements, whereas the [East] Indian is said to prefer larger, delayed reinforcements.' This article describes the study and discusses its results.

333 **Plural and differential acculturation in Trinidad.**

Daniel J. Crowley. *American Anthropologist*, vol. 59, no. 5 (Oct. 1957), p. 817-24. bibliog.

A scholarly paper, based on material collected in connection with the Local Studies Programme, Trinidad Extra-Mural Department, University College of the West Indies. Crowley states that he 'will attempt to show some of the means by which Trinidadians of diverse origins have managed to adjust to their complex social situation without losing their subcultural identities.' Crowley enumerates the thirteen vertical rungs of Trinidad's social ladder as of the 1950s, from the foreign whites ('Bekes') at the top to the low-caste Hindu East Indians at the bottom. He then explains how all these separate groups are at least partially acculturated or 'Creolized,' and are in 'basic agreement in such vital areas as language, folk belief, magic practice, mating and family structure, festivals, and music, [which] provide the common ground for Trinidad to function as a society.' Members of each group both learn and utilize ways of other groups without feeling any inconsistency.

Family, marriage, mating patterns and kinship

334 **Women as heads of households in the Caribbean: family structure and feminine status.**

Joycelin Massiah. New York: UNESCO, 1983. 69p. bibliog.

Twenty-seven per cent of Trinidad and Tobago's households are headed by women. (In the Caribbean area as a whole, thirty-two per cent of the households have female heads.) Massiah presents valuable comparative statistical data on this type of family organization as it is found in the region, profiling the female household head – her education, employment, and occupation – and describing her survival strategies. The article also provides information on the public benefits and financial assistance available to female-headed households.

335 **Marital careers in Trinidad.**

Patricia Voydanoff, Hyman Rodman. *Journal of Marriage and the Family*, vol. 40, no. 1 (Feb. 1978), p. 157-63. bibliog.

'Data presented on the marital careers of 1976 lower-class respondents in a non-probability sample.' The authors classify Trinidadian mating unions as 'friending,' 'living,' and legally married and study the pattern of shifts between the three types.

336 **Sexual politics in the East Indian family in Trinidad.**

Michael V. Angrosino. *Caribbean Studies*, vol. 16, no. 1 (April 1976), p. 44-66.

Based on data collected in Zenobia, an East Indian village in Trinidad in 1970-1971 and 1973, this analysis of the Indian family examines the pattern of dominant-subordinate relationships within the family group, emphasizing the role played in the family system by the subjugation of the daughter-in-law. Angrosino discusses the Indian family in estate and post-estate days, noting changes in family style and the implications of such changes. He sees the Indian family in Trinidad as about to enter upon a third phase of development, initiated by different interpretations of the role of the bride.

337 **Transformation of African and Indian family traditions in the southern Caribbean.**

John Stuart MacDonald, Leatrice D. MacDonald. *Comparative Studies in Society and History*, vol. 15, no. 2 (March 1973), p. 171-98. bibliog.

Trinidad and Tobago is focused on in this examination of whether or not there is a direct connection between agricultural organization and family-household structure. Contrasts are made between the situation obtaining among Blacks and that obtaining among East Indians. 'The Negro family ideology of the southern Caribbean was formed because of slavery and semi-paternalistic peonage, while the East Indian family ideology was formed despite bondage in bureaucratic agriculture.'

338 **Structural imbalances of gratification: the case of the Caribbean mating system.**

Morris Freilich, Lewis A. Coser. *British Journal of Sociology*, vol. 23, no. 1 (March 1972), p. 1-19.

The authors describe and analyse the sex life of Black peasants in the community of Anamat in eastern Trinidad, in order to 'reveal how a social system that is based on complementarity between sexual partners nevertheless presents such asymmetry that its equilibrium is extremely precarious.'

339 **Lower-class families: the culture of poverty in negro Trinidad.**
Hyman Rodman. London, New York: Oxford University Press, 1971. 242p.

A detailed ethnographic description of 'lower-class family life within a community,' as well as an attempt to be explanatory 'as a first step toward a general theoretical statement of lower-class family organization.' The study is the result of eleven months of fieldwork in a Black rural village in northeastern Trinidad (pseudonymously called 'Coconut Village'), in 1956, 1959, 1962, and 1968. There are chapters on historical background, family relationships, family life, and theories of lower class values. Appendixes are entitled: 'Calypso selections,' and 'Glossary of Trinidad Creole English terms.'

340 **Residential segregation and intermarriage in San Fernando, Trinidad.**
Colin G. Clarke. *Geographical Review*, vol. 61, no. 2 (April 1971), p. 198-218. maps.

'The present study examines selected patterns of association among the Creoles and East Indians in San Fernando, the second largest town in Trinidad. The major racial and religious components of the population are identified [and] their distributions and spatial associations considered. A sample of households [is] analyzed to assess the frequency of intermarriage and the homogeneity of domestic units.' Based on data from the study, Clarke concludes that there is a lack of intermarriage in San Fernando: 'the Creoles and the East Indians – Hindu, Muslim, and Christian – are all endogamous with respect to both racial and religious criteria.' Maps of the racial distribution of San Fernando's population accompany the text.

341 **Marriage and family differences among lower-class Negro and East Indian women in Trinidad.**
Robert R. Bell. *Race*, vol. 12, no. 1 (July 1970), p. 59-73. bibliog.

Professor Bell reports the results of a study carried out in 1969 in a rural area of central Trinidad, not far from San Fernando. A questionnaire was administered to 200 Black and 100 East Indian women. Replies to the questionnaire indicated a number of sharp differences between the two groups in their views and practices in regard to marriage, marital sex, parenthood, illegitimacy, and child-rearing.

342 **Fidelity and forms of marriage: the consensual union in the Caribbean.**
Hyman Rodman. In: *Extramarital relations*. Edited by Gerhard Neubeck. Englewood Cliffs, New Jersey: Prentice-Hall, 1969, p. 94-107. bibliog.

Rodman uses 'the literature on marriage as a process, and on alternate forms of marriage in order to help clarify the disputed status of consensual unions in the Caribbean.' He focuses on the principle of fidelity in order to ascertain whether such unions are normative or deviant within the Caribbean lower classes. Data is presented that was gathered from Trinidadian respondents expressing their attitudes toward infidelity within varying mating relationships: consensual union ('living'), non-cohabiting sexual relationship ('friending'), and conventional marriage.

343 **Sex, secrets and systems.**

Morris Freilich. In: *Proceedings of the conference on the family in the Caribbean, I., St. Thomas, Virgin Islands, 1968.* Edited by Stanford N. Gerber. Rio Piedras, Puerto Rico: University of Puerto Rico, Institute of Caribbean Studies, 1968, p. 47-62. bibliog.

A systems analysis of the sexual life of Black peasants in a farming community in Eastern Trinidad. Frielich describes and interprets the 'sex-fame' game.

344 **Illegitimacy in the Caribbean social structure: a reconsideration.**

Hyman Rodman. *American Sociological Review*, vol. 31, no. 5 (Oct. 1966), p. 673-83.

Based on research undertaken in Trinidad in 1962, Rodman presents new evidence in regard to the view of non-legal sexual unions and illegitimate children held by the Caribbean lower class. Rodman claims that 'the normative pattern [of marriage and children] within the lower class has been stretched so that, in addition to subscribing to the middle-class ideals . . . [the lower class has] also come to subscribe to the pattern of non-legal unions and illegitimate children.' His conclusions are derived from the replies of ninety-seven men and seventy-nine women to a questionnaire designed to determine the percentage – by sex and class – favouring non-legal unions.

345 **Patterns of East Indian family organization in Trinidad.**

Barton M. Schwartz. *Caribbean Studies*, vol. 5, no. 1 (April 1965), p. 23-36.

A close analysis of the Hindu residents and their family system in the pseudonymous 'Boodram,' a mainly East Indian village in southwestern Trinidad. Schwartz's goals in the study were 'to learn which institutions are most vital and basic to the general structure of Indian society,' and 'to expose some of the major factors involved in the structural adaptation of the East Indian family in Trinidad.' Schwartz finds that in Trinidad the traditional Indian extended family has lost ground to the nuclear family.

346 **The East Indian family overseas.**

Leo David. *Social and Economic Studies*, vol. 13, no. 3 (Sept. 1964), p. 383-96. bibliog.

Although Trinidad is mentioned only in passing in this article, David's examination of what has happened to the Hindu family of Northern India when transplanted to other societies will be of interest to those studying the East Indians of Trinidad. David looks at marriage phenomena, behaviour in the Indian household, and certain other aspects of Hinduism such as ritual and caste. The traditional family pattern, which is prevalent in India, is described and the extent to which shifts in this pattern have occurred in overseas Indian communities are discussed.

347 **Caste and endogamy in Trinidad.**
Barton M. Schwartz. *Southwestern Journal of Anthropology*, vol. 20, no. 1 (Spring 1964), p. 58-66. bibliog.

Schwartz analyses marriage patterns among East Indians in Trinidad by studying the caste institution as it obtains in the pseudonymous 'Boodram,' a village with an almost entirely Hindu population. His article explores significant marital trends by group affiliation among the inhabitants of 'Boodram.' The article is based upon fieldwork conducted in Trinidad in 1961.

348 **Mating among East Indian and non-Indian women in Trinidad.**
G. W. Roberts, L. Braithwaite. *Social and Economic Studies*, vol. 11, no. 3 (Sept. 1962), p. 203-40.

A quantitative study comparing the mating patterns of women of two broad racial groups. Sexual unions are classified into three types: visiting, common law, and married. The authors utilize data from a sample survey conducted in Trinidad in 1958.

349 **Serial polygyny, negro peasants, and model analysis.**
Morris Freilich. *American Anthropologist*, vol. 63, no. 5 pt. 1 (Oct. 1961), p. 955-75. bibliog.

Using a systems approach, Freilich constructs a model of Black mating practices and the Black family based on data collected in 1957-1958 in an eleven-month study of Anamat, an ethnically mixed village in eastern Trinidad. After a general description of the Anamat community, Freilich provides details regarding the membership groups, sex life, time orientation, authority patterns, and the sentiments and symbols of its Black residents. Freilich then compares his model of Anamat to African, lower class proletarian, and plantation-slave mating and family systems, and finds the Anamat model closest to the plantation-slave system.

350 **Marital relations in a Trinidad village.**
Hyman Rodman. *Marriage and Family Living*, vol. 23, no. 2 (May 1961), p. 166-70.

Rodman describes three different kinds of marital or quasi-marital relationships – 'friending', 'living', and married – that obtain in a lower class Black village in Trinidad, and attempts to account for the relative frequency of these relationships. The mores relating to each relationship are described and discussed. Rodman points out that 'fluidity' is the essence of marital life in the pseudonymous 'Coconut Village': 'fluid' mating patterns are 'functional in that they provide the lower-class person with acceptable alternatives [to legal matrimony] that permit him to live with both his conscience and his economic uncertainty.'

351 **A gross mating table for a West Indian population.**
G. W. Roberts, Lloyd Braithwaite. *Population Studies*, vol. 14, no. 3 (Jan. 1961), p. 198-217.

A gross mating table is used to present a summary of the mating habits of non-East Indian Trinidadian women over forty-five years of age who took part in a small scale sample survey in 1958. Data on frequency and types of unions – visiting, common law, and married are noted.

352 **Fertility differentials by family type in Trinidad.**
G. W. Roberts, Lloyd Braithwaite. *Annals of the New York Academy of Sciences*, vol. 84, art. 17 (Dec. 8, 1960), p. 963-80.

Based on material collected in a survey in Trinidad in 1958, this study correlates child-bearing with the three types of mating unions found in Trinidad – formal marriage, common law union, and 'visiting' union.

353 **Illegitimacy in the Caribbean.**
William J. Goode. *American Sociological Review*, vol. 25, no. 1 (Feb. 1960), p. 21-30.

Trinidad is briefly mentioned in this discussion of the values, norms, and social practices relating to illegitimacy that obtain among the peoples of the Caribbean area.

354 **Crisis of the West Indian family; a sample study.**
Dom Basil Matthews. N.p.: Extra Mural Department, University College of the West Indies, 1953. bibliog. Reprinted, Westport, Connecticut: Greenwood Press, 1971. 117p.

This study by a Trinidadian Roman Catholic priest focuses on the common law marriage or non-legal union among Blacks in Trinidad. Based on field work, interviews, and historical documents in Trinidad.

Women

355 **Trinidad women speak.**
Edited by Bori S. Clark, with an introduction by Patricia Mohammed. Redlands, California: Libros Latinos, 1981. 71p.

Presents interviews with Trinidadian women that focus on questions of social conditions and race relations.

356 **Women in the Caribbean: a bibliography.**
Bertie A. Cohen Stuart. Leiden, The Netherlands: Department of Caribbean Studies, Royal Institute of Linguistics and Anthropology, 1979. 163p.

A list of 651 annotated references, covering family and household, cultural factors, education, economic factors, and politics and law as they relate to the women of the Caribbean islands.

357 **The status of women in Caribbean societies: an overview of their social, economic and sexual roles.**
Frances Henry, Pamela Wilson. *Social and Economic Studies*, vol. 24, no. 2 (June 1975), p. 165-99.

An extensive review of the published research literature on the women of the Caribbean region.

Social Welfare and Social Problems

General

358 **Servol and its education and community development programmes in Trinidad and Tobago: an observation.**
Angela Morrison. Langholm, Dumfriesshire, Scotland: Arkleton Trust, 1983. 69p. maps.

A look at the Servol organization, which is comprised of volunteer social service workers, and its programmes in Trinidad and Tobago.

359 **Social Security Programs Throughout the World, 1979.**
Office of Research and Statistics, Office of International Policy, Social Security Administration, US Department of Health and Human Services. Washington, DC: Government Printing Office, 1980. Revised May 1980. 267p. (Research Report, no. 54; SSA Publication, no. 13-11805).

Prepared by the Comparative Studies Staff of the Office of International Policy, this publication has been issued periodically by the United States Social Security Administration since 1937. The volume reviewed here updates the edition of December 1973. Its purpose is 'to assist those interested in comparing social security systems on an international basis.' Data is presented in tabular form, with brief discussions of the sources from which the information is drawn. The Trinidad and Tobago section, on p. 240-41, covers the social security system of that country: the source of funds, qualifying conditions for benefits, cash benefits for temporary and permanent disability, survivor benefits, medical benefits for dependents, and the administrative organization of the programme.

360 **Community development in Trinidad and Tobago 1943-1973; from welfare to patronage.**
Susan E. Craig. Mona, Jamaica: Institute of Social and Economic Research, University of the West Indies, 1974. 138p. map. bibliog. (Working Paper. Institute of Social and Economic Research. University of the West Indies, no. 4).

Craig examines state activity in the field of community development during a thirty-year period, tracing the history of social welfare and government policies and practices.

Family planning

361 **Changes in the use of birth control methods.**
Jack Harewood. *Population Studies*, vol. 27, no. 1 (March 1973), p. 33-56.

Based on data on contraception and on changes in contraception methods by women in Trinidad, that was collected in a survey conducted during 1970 and 1971. The paper first describes the fertility situation and the family planning programme in Trinidad and Tobago, and goes on to provide data on the survey itself. The main body of the article contains Harewood's analysis of contraceptive histories. The text is supplemented with the presentation of the data in tabular form.

362 **Family planning dropouts in Trinidad: report of a small study.**
Jack Reynolds. *Social and Economic Studies*, vol. 20, no. 2 (June 1971), p. 176-87.

A study was conducted in 1969 to investigate why women who had attended clinics sponsored by the National Family Planning Programme (NFPP) of Trinidad and Tobago were no longer attending the clinics, and whether or not they were still using contraception. This article summarizes the results of the complete study. The most important finding seems to be that women who drop out of the NFPP tend to drop out of contraception altogether.

363 **Politics and population in the Caribbean.**
Aaron Segal, with the assistance of Kent C. Earnhardt. Rio Piedras, Puerto Rico: Institute of Caribbean Studies, University of Puerto Rico, 1969. 158 [55]p. bibliog. (Special Study, no. 7).

Based on research conducted in 1966-1967, this monograph covers the entire Caribbean area with separate sections on individual countries. Trinidad and Tobago's population policy is covered on p. 59-67. The central government has endorsed the goal of reducing the dual-island-nation's fertility rate.

Alcoholism

364 **Drinking patterns and alcoholism in Trinidad.**
Carole Yawney. In: *Beliefs, behavior, and alcoholic beverages; a cross-cultural survey.* Edited by Mac Marshall. Ann Arbor, Michigan: University of Michigan Press, 1979, p. 94-107.

Contrasts are drawn between East Indian (Hindu) and Black drinking patterns in Trinidad.

365 **Treatment of alcoholism in Trinidad and Tobago, 1956-65.**
M. H. Beaubrun. *British Journal of Psychiatry*, vol. 113, no. 499 (June 1967), p. 643-58. bibliog.

This article describes and evaluates an alcoholism treatment programme in Trinidad and Tobago. 'The programme, initiated by the author in 1956, combined emetine aversion treatment in a group setting, with milieu therapy and group psychotherapy of a didactic kind aimed at producing conversion (rather than aversion) to uncritical belief in the tenets of Alcoholics Anonymous.'

Crime, criminology and justice

366 **Gene Miles, our national heroine.**
Nyahuma Obiku. Port-of-Spain: Caribbean Historical Society, 1982. 64p. bibliog.

A biographical tribute to the civil servant who was instrumental in exposing the Gas Station Racket in 1966.

367 **Rape and socio-economic conditions in Trinidad and Tobago.**
Kenneth Pryce, Daurius Figueira. In: *Crime and punishment in the Caribbean.* Edited and introduced by Rosemary Brana-Shute, Gary Brana-Shute. Gainesville, Florida: Center for Latin American Studies, University of Florida, 1980, p. 58-75. map. bibliog.

This analysis views rape in Trinidad and Tobago as a structurally-produced problem. 'This paper . . . is largely an attempt to make sense of the so-called "rape problem" in Trinidad and Tobago. After a consideration of evidence revealing the high incidence of the offence in the depressed urban areas of county St. George, the paper argues that, though certainly "bizarre," rape in low-income communities in Trinidad and Tobago is not necessarily the product of a "sick" mind, but is an expressive response by lower class males to the destruction of manhood under capitalist and sexist conditions where conventional avenues of masculine expression are non-existent.'

368 **The return of Eva Peron; with the killings in Trinidad.**
V. S. Naipaul. New York: Knopf, 1980. 227p.

Early in 1972, Michael de Freitas, the self-styled Black Power revolutionary also known as Michael X and Michael Abdul Malik, along with several other members of his 'commune' killed Gail Ann Benson and Joe Skerritt. De Freitas was tried, convicted, and hanged for the murders. In a lengthy essay in this volume, 'Michael X and the Black Power killings in Trinidad' (p. 3-91), Naipaul narrates the grim tale of these murders, setting them against a background of racial obsession and tormented fantasies of power.

369 **A historical account of the Trinidad and Tobago police force from the earliest times.**
C. R. Ottley. Trinidad: The Author, 1964. 152p.

The only available account of the history of Trinidad and Tobago's police force.

370 **The murders of Boysie Singh; robber, arsonist, pirate, mass-murderer, vice and gambling king of Trinidad.**
Derek Bickerton. London: A. Barker, 1962. 230p.

Recounts the life and criminal career of John 'Boysie' Singh (1908-1957).

Racial discrimination and racial antagonism

371 **Racial discrimination in employment in Trinidad and Tobago (based on data from the 1960 census).**
Jack Harewood. *Social and Economic Studies*, vol. 20, no. 3 (Sept. 1971), p. 267-93.

'This paper . . . is intended mainly as background information for the more extensive study of this problem being undertaken by the University of the West Indies.' Harewood provides a complete picture of the employed as indicated by data collected in the 1960 census. However, he does not give a direct yes or no answer to the question of whether or not there is racial discrimination in employment in Trinidad.

372 **Racial discrimination in employment in the private sector in Trinidad and Tobago: a study of the business elite and the social structure.**
Acton Camejo. *Social and Economic Studies*, vol. 20, no. 3 (Sept. 1971), p. 294-318. bibliog.

This exploratory study investigates whether 'there was possible racial discrimination in the hiring of persons for the most preferred or top occupations – Executive,

Administrative, or Municipal –' in private business organizations in Trinidad and Tobago.

373 **Culture, politics and race relations.**
Vera Rubin. *Social and Economic Studies*, vol. 11, no. 4 (Dec. 1962), p. 433-55.

An examination of race relations and the ideology of race, based on data derived from studies undertaken in Trinidad in 1957 and 1961. These studies found much racial stereotyping and revealed that a high level of mutual antagonism exists between racial groups in Trinidad.

Suicide

374 **Socio-cultural aspects of attempted suicide among women in Trinidad and Tobago.**
Aggrey W. Burke. *British Journal of Psychiatry*, vol. 125 (Oct. 1974), p. 347-74. bibliog.

A study to investigate whether or not suicide attempts by Trinidadian females were more frequent among women of East Indian origin residing in rural areas than among urban women of African descent. Case notes on women admitted to a psychiatric unit during a twelve-week period were examined. No difference in ethnic distribution was found among patients who had attempted suicide, although those of East Indian origin tended to be older.

375 **Clinic aspects of attempted suicide among women in Trinidad and Tobago.**
Aggrey W. Burke. *British Journal of Psychiatry*, vol. 125 (August 1974), p. 175-76. bibliog.

'This paper describes the distribution of female attempted suicide and other psychiatric admissions in the twenty-bedded Psychiatric Unit of Trinidad and Tobago' during one period, 1 June 1969 to 31 May 1970. Out of 350 female patients, 90 (26 per cent) were admitted on account of a suicide attempt.

Politics and Government

376 **The Commonwealth Caribbean and the contemporary world order: the cases of Jamaica and Trinidad.**
Paul W. Ashley. In: *The newer Caribbean; decolonization, democracy and development.* Edited by Paget Henry, Carl Stone. Philadelphia: Institute for the Study of Human Issues, 1982, p. 159-70. (Inter-American Politics Series, no. 4).

An analysis of the political economy of two Caribbean countries that seeks 'to explore comparatively the impact of the international order on the process of national development in both of these island states. In particular, the patterns of penetration, the specific adaptations and constraints, and the overall significance for the development of democratic institutions will be highlighted.' Ashley sees the two states as caught in a dilemma: they have to rely on private foreign capital for necessary growth in the economy, although this pattern of dependency is perpetuating conditions which can be considered inimical to natural development, which in its turn bears on the survival, the development or the demise of democratic institutions in the two nations.

377 **Movement of the people; essays on independence.**
Selwyn R. Cudjoe. Ithaca, New York: Calaloux Publications, 1983. 217p.

Essays on the politics, government, and social conditions of post-1962 Trinidad and Tobago.

378 **Personalization of power in an elected government; Eric Williams and Trinidad and Tobago, 1973-1981.**
Carl D. Parris. *Journal of Interamerican Studies and World Affairs*, vol. 25, no. 2 (May 1983), p. 171-91. bibliog.

'A study of the structure of political power in a context of political illegitimacy and spectacular economic growth.' Parris notes the 'strategies used by the prime minister of Trinidad and Tobago to arrest the continuing process of delegitimization that had set into the political system' while at the same time a process of power concentration was going on. He concludes: 'The political profile that emerges is one of liberal capitalism, a phenomenon not normally associated with developing countries. The economic profile is vastly different, with a high degree of state ownership of some sectors interlocked with party political control.'

379 **Resource ownership and the prospects for democracy: the case of Trinidad and Tobago.**
Carl D. Parris. In: *The newer Caribbean; decolonization, democracy, and development.* Edited by Paget Henry, Carl Stone. Philadelphia: Institute for the Study of Human Issues, 1982, p. 313-26. (Inter-American Politics Series, no. 4).

Parris examines the interrelationship between resource ownership and the continuation of democratic processes in Trinidad and Tobago, exploring the government's attitude to resource ownership; the model of development, namely modernization, chosen by the government; and the consequences of this choice, particularly its implications for democracy. He sees a possibility for the emergence of a 'strong regime' in Trinidad where he believes 'the whole base of a democratic political system has withered away.'

380 **Black intellectuals and the dilemmas of race and class in Trinidad.**
Ivar Oxaal. Cambridge, Massachusetts: Schenkman Publishing, 1982. 334p.

A single-volume reprint of two of Oxaal's books on Black Power politics in Trinidad: *Black intellectuals come to power; the rise of Creole nationalism in Trinidad & Tobago* (1968), which traces the events leading to Trinidad's independence; and *Race and revolutionary consciousness: a documentary interpretation of the 1970 black power revolt in Trinidad* (1971), which deals with the February 1970 disturbances. This latest edition adds an epilogue on the final years of the Eric Williams era, 1971-1981.

381 **Eric Williams: the man, his ideas, and his politics: a study of political power.**
Ramesh Deosaran. Port-of-Spain: Signum, 1981. 194p. bibliog.

A biography of independent Trinidad and Tobago's first Prime Minister.

382 **Notes and comments: Afro-Indian relations in Trinidad and Tobago: an assessment.**
John Gaffar LaGuerre. *Social and Economic Studies*, vol. 25, no. 3 (Sept. 1976), p. 291-306.

A good summary article that traces the path of Afro-Indian relations from the 19th century to the present, pointing out the interaction of history, economics, and politics in the relationship between the two groups. Also included is an interesting discussion of the approaches taken to the study of the East Indians by scholars of various disciplines and intellectual orientations.

383 **Documents from the National United Freedom Fighters of Trinidad.**
[No author.] *Pan-African Journal*, vol. 8, no. (Summer 1975), 203-25.

This collection of documents prepared by the National United Freedom Fighters (NUFF), a leftist guerrilla organization in Trinidad, consists of an essay entitled 'On the question of ideology in the name of God and all the people', an interview with several unnamed members of the group, and a letter by Terence Thornhill, secretary of the People's Freedom Committee.

384 **Politics and Afro-Indian relations in Trinidad.**
Brinsley Samaroo. In: *Calcutta to Caroni: the East Indians of Trinidad.* Edited by John Gaffar La Guerre. Port-of-Spain: Longmans Caribbean, 1974, p. 84-97.

A history of attempts at Afro-Indian solidarity, particularly during the 1930s.

385 **Through a maze of colour.**
Albert Gomes. Port-of-Spain: Key Caribbean Publications, 1974. 251p.

The autobiography of the Trinidadian political figure Albert Gomes (1911- .). Gordon K. Lewis calls the book 'a frank discussion of life and labor in the Byzantine politics of the Trinidad picaroon society over the last forty years.'

386 **The case of the missing majority.**
Ken I. Boodhoo. *Caribbean Review*, vol. 6, no. 2 (April-May-June 1974), p. 3-7).

A discussion of the political situation in the early 1970s in Trinidad and Tobago and Guyana. 'Since no group in either the Trinidad or the Guyanese societies has a monopoly over power, these societies are comprised largely of "minority groups".'

387 **Black power in the Caribbean context.**
David Lowenthal. *Economic Geography*, vol. 48, no. 1 (Jan. 1972), p. 116-34. bibliog.

Examines the paradox of Black dissatisfaction in primarily Black societies, noting the racial complexities of West Indian societies and that 'formal independence and equality have scarcely altered West Indian social structure.' Lowenthal points out that economic stresses in the Caribbean are often experienced in racial terms. He discusses the roles played in the Caribbean by foreign Whites, local Whites, the coloured middle class, and the black majority, and touches on the themes of authoritarianism and repression, Black Power agitation, black political and cultural movements, Blacks vs. East Indians, and the problem of West Indian cultural identity. Examples from Trinidad are given.

388 **C. L. R. James and the race/class question.**
Tony Martin. *Race*, vol. 14, no. 2 (Oct. 1972), p. 183-83.

A discussion of the black Trinidadian Marxist intellectual's position on the relative weight to be assigned to race and class as key factors in the struggle of Blacks for freedom from colonialism and racial prejudice. James, true to his Marxism, stressed the primacy of class. Martin's article includes a biographical sketch of James, highlighting his influence on Pan-Africanism.

389 **Race and nationalism in Trinidad and Tobago: a study of decolonization in a multiracial society.**
Selwyn D. Ryan. Toronto: University of Toronto Press, 1972. 509p. maps.

A major study of the transition of Trinidad and Tobago from a British colony to an independent nation. The author's emphasis is on the influence that the island's cultural and ethnic diversity has had on the struggle for political and social reform. Part one (1797-1955) provides the historical background of the period of British rule; Part two (1955-1956) covers the rise of the People's National Movement (PNM); Part three (1956-1962) deals with the PNM's consolidation of its power and its conflict with the Hindu Democratic Labour Party (DLP); and Part four (1962-1971) evaluates the achievements of the PNM in terms of its goals of 1956.

390 **East Indians and Black Power in Trinidad.**
David G. Nicholls. *Race*, vol. 12, no. 4 (April 1971), p. 443-59.

An examination of 'the actions and ideas of Black Power leaders in Trinidad during the crisis of February-April 1970, with particular reference to the problem of East Indian participation in the movement.' The reactions of various groups of Indians to the events of these months are noted.

391 **East Indians in Trinidad: a study in minority politics.**
Yogendra K. Malik. London, New York: Published for the Institute of Race Relations by Oxford University Press, 1971. 199p. bibliog.

An investigation of Trinidad's East Indians as a political, rather than a sociological or anthropological phenomenon. Malik traces the events leading to the formation and the development of the Democratic Labour Party (DLP), formerly the 'East Indian' party of Trinidad. His focus is on the East Indian élite; the data upon which his book is based was gathered through structured interviews which he conducted with eighty-nine members of this class.

392 **Black Power and the Caribbean: 1.**
A Special Correspondent. *Race Today*, vol. 2, no. 11 (Nov. 1970), p. 403-05. map.

This journalistic piece on the factors contributing to political tension in the Caribbean, written by a correspondent recently returned from the area, focuses on Trinidad and Tobago. The author comments on the Black Power rioting and racial disorder of February, 1970, which destroyed the myth of 'all-ah-we-is-one' harmony in the island state. He then advances some possible reasons for the outbreak of violent social protest in the country, and discusses Trinidad-born Stokely Carmichael's equation of Black Power with Pan-Africanism.

393 **Power to the Caribbean people.**
V. S. Naipaul. *New York Review of Books*, vol. 15, no. 4 (3 Sept. 1970), p. 32-34.

Naipaul is sharply critical of Black Power in the Caribbean context, seeing the movement as a fantasy bred by the helplessness and isolation of the islands, which he characterizes as 'manufactured societies . . . where nothing was generated locally.'

394 **Inward hunger; the education of a prime minister.**
Eric Williams, with an introduction by Sir Denis Brogan. London: Deutsch 1969. Reprinted, Chicago: University of Chicago Press, 1971. 352p.

This autobiography of the Black scholar-politician-statesman is required reading for students of Trinidadian politics and the People's National Movement. Williams gives his readers a portrait of himself as a public figure, tracing his intellectual and political development to 1968.

395 **Trinidad electoral politics: the persistence of the race factor.**
Krishna Bahadoorsingh. London: Institute for Race Relations, 1968. 98p. bibliog. (Institute of Race Relations. Special Series).

Bahadoorsingh selected three racially-contrasting Trinidadian electoral districts – Laventille (Black), Naparima (East Indian), and Fyzabad (mixed) – and analysed voting behaviour in these districts during the 1956 and 1961 elections. His results point to race as the crucial factor in the elections.

396 **The Senate of Trinidad and Tobago.**
Ann Spackman. *Social and Economic Studies*, vol. 16, no. 1 (March 1967), p. 77-100.

An article written in 1965-1966 that considers the role and function of the political institution of the Senate of Trinidad and Tobago, as established in 1961. 'Its legal powers are defined in the Constitution but its real position and function in the political life of the country are still to be clarified.' Spackman first looks at the composition of the legislative body and the social and economic backgrounds of its members; she then considers 'the function of the Senate and what the Senators themselves think of the effectiveness of their branch of the legislature.'

Constitution, Law and Human Rights

Constitution

397 **West Indian constitutions: post-independence reform.**
Sir Fred Phillips. New York, London, Rome: Oceana Publications, 1985. 370p. bibliog.

In Chapter four, 'Constitutional developments in the republic of Trinidad & Tobago and post-independence relations between the partners' (p. 95-114), Phillips provides a historical overview of the union of the two islands, then discusses 'some novel [constitutional] developments affecting Tobago as the junior partner in the unitary state.' In other chapters, the independence of Trinidad and Tobago's judiciary receives attention, leading constitutional cases are highlighted, and the constitutional provisions relating to the appointment, functions, and removal from office of the nation's Head of State are considered.

398 **Freedom in the Caribbean: a study in constitutional change.**
Sir Fred Phillips, with a foreword by E. V. Luckhoo. New York: Oceana Publications, 1977. 737p. bibliog.

Chapter thirteen of this hefty volume, 'The first general review of an Independence Constitution: republican status for Trinidad and Tobago,' discusses the Report of the Wooding Constitutional Commission and summarizes its main recommendations for the reform of the nation's Independence Constitution. Relevant documents, including the 1976 Constitution that is now in force in the country, are provided in their entirety in appendixes to the volume: Appendix thirteen provides a 'Summary of recommendations of the Wooding Constitutional Commission for Trinidad and Tobago on constitutional reform in the country'; and Appendix fourteen studies 'The constitution for the republic of Trinidad and Tobago act, 1976 (Act no. 4 of 1976).'

399 **The making of the 1946 constitution in Trinidad.**
Brinsley Samaroo. *Caribbean Studies*, vol. 15, no. 4 (Jan. 1976), p. 5-27.

'This article seeks to describe the attitudes of the various participant groups in the government for constitutional change, to focus attention on the debate that characterized the making of the 1946 constitution, and to point out some of the consequences of this debate.'

400 **Constitutional development in Trinidad & Tobago.**
Ann Spackman. *Social and Economic Studies*, vol. 14, no. 4 (Dec. 1965), p. 283-320.

A valuable, detailed account of the discussions leading to the Independence Constitution of 1962. After an introductory sketch of changes in constitutional form in the country prior to 1956, Spackman concentrates her analysis on the development of the Trinidad and Tobago constitution from 1956 up to the granting of independence in 1962.

401 **The constitutional history of Trinidad & Tobago.**
H. O. B. Wooding. *Caribbean Quarterly*, vol. 6, nos. 3-4 (May 1960), p. 143-76.

A transcription of a lecture which discusses the various documents according to which Trinidad had been governed, from the Spanish Cedula of 1783 to the Constitution of 1956. Constitutional history is explained and placed in the context of historical events and political forces. Wooding includes mention of the 1797 Treaty of Capitulation by which Trinidad became a British possession, the system of Crown Colony government in force during the 19th century, and the introduction of representative government through legislative elections in 1925.

402 **1959 – summary of constitutional advances: (a) Trinidad and Tobago.**
Harvey da Costa. *Caribbean Quarterly*, vol. 6, nos. 3-4 (May 1960), p. 230.

A summary of the principal changes contained in 'The Trinidad and Tobago (Constitution) (Amendment) Order in Council, 1959.'

Law and legislation

403 **The background of the legislation of non-Christian marriages in Trinidad and Tobago.**
J. C. Jha. In: *East Indians in the Caribbean; colonialism and the struggle for identity: papers presented to a symposium on East Indians in the Caribbean, the University of the West Indies, June, 1975.* Preface by Bridget Brereton, Winston Dookeran, with an introduction by V. S. Naipaul. Millwood, New York, London; Nendeln, Liechtenstein: Kraus International, 1982, p. 117-39.

'In 1945, a century after the first group of indentured Indian labourers landed in Port of Spain, and one decade before a Hindu Marriage Act was passed in India, the Legislative Council of Trinidad and Tobago passed the Hindu Marriage Ordinance. One decade prior to this the Muslim Marriage Ordinance was passed.' Jha's detailed and informative presentation clarifies the thinking and events that led to this legislation.

404 **Statutory regulation of collective bargaining: with special reference to the Industrial Relations Act of Trinidad and Tobago.**
Chuks Okpaluba. Mona, Jamaica: Institute of Social and Economic Research, University of the West Indies, 1975. 183p. bibliog. (Law and Society in the Caribbean, no. 5).

The major part of this volume analyses the legal implications of the Industrial Relations Act of 1972. Okpaluba also includes a discussion of the effects of the provisions of this legislation on the individual worker. Other pertinent labour legislation in the British Caribbean is also referred to.

405 **The law and cannabis in the West Indies.**
H. Aubrey Fraser. *Social and Economic Studies*, vol. 23, no. 3 (Sept. 1974), p. 361-85.

An article on current legislation regarding cannabis in the English-speaking countries in or near the Caribbean. The substance, known as ganja in the region, was first brought to the Caribbean in the mid-19th century by East Indian indentured labourers. It was first legislated against in Trinidad by the Ganja Ordinance of 1916. Current Trinidadian legislation in regard to cannabis is described in the article, and police statistics on cannabis use, from 1966 to 1973, are given.

406 **A bibliographical guide to law in the Commonwealth Caribbean.**
Keith Patchett, Valerie Jenkins. Mona, Jamaica: Institute of Social and Economic Research, University of the West Indies, 1973. 80p. (Law and Society in the Caribbean, no. 2).

'Brings together comprehensive information on source material of interest to students and practitioners of law in the Commonwealth Caribbean. The entries are arranged under geographical and subject headings and an author and subject index is provided.'

407 **West Indian land laws: conspectus and reform.**
O. R. Marshall. *Social and Economic Studies*, vol. 20, no. 1 (March 1971), p. 1-14.

Covers some aspects of the land laws of British Caribbean nations – Trinidad and Tobago included – where the basis of the land law is the English common law. The author notes that 'the Englishness of West Indian land law [fails] to take into account the realities of the socio-economic situation' and the accepted patterns of Caribbean family and social structure.

Human rights

408 **Trinidad and Tobago.**
In: *Country reports on human rights practices for 1983; report submitted to the Committee on Foreign Affairs, U.S. House of Representatives, and the Committee on Foreign Relations, U.S. Senate.* U.S. State Department. Washington, DC: US Government Printing Office, 1984, p. 700-04.

Country reports on human rights practices are based on information furnished by US diplomatic missions abroad, by congressional studies, non-governmental organizations, and by the human rights bodies of international organizations. This report covers conditions to the end of 1983 and the beginning of 1984. The human rights situation in Trinidad and Tobago is generally good: there are no political prisoners and the government is responsive to criticism.

409 **The East Indians of Guyana and Trinidad.**
Malcolm Cross. London, New York: Minority Rights Group, 1980. 18p. (Report: Minority Rights Group, no. 13).

A brief report by an international human rights group that investigates discrimination and prejudice. This report was first published in 1972 and reissued with revisions in 1980.

Administration and Local Government

410 **The ecology of development administration in Jamaica, Trinidad and Tobago, and Barbados.**
Jean-Claude Garcia-Zamor. N.p.: Program of Development Financing, General Secretariat, Organization of American States, 1977. 122p. bibliog.

A work by an American trained Haitian scholar that relates the development process to the socio-economic political environment in three Caribbean countries. Garcia-Zamor deals with both theoretical concepts and particular examples in his examination of the bureaucracies of the three nations. A critical review of this book by W. Errol Bowen of the Institute of Social and Economic Research, University of the West Indies, Mona, Jamaica, appears in *Caribbean Quarterly*, vol. 26, no. 3 (Sept. 1980), p. 53-56.

411 **Issues and problems in Caribbean public administration: a reader.**
Edited by Selwyn Ryan. St. Augustine, Trinidad: Department of Government, University of the West Indies, 1977. 2 vols.

This selection of documents gathered together for the use of students of public administration, includes much material from Trinidad.

412 **Local democracy in the Commonwealth Caribbean: a study of adaptation and growth.**
Paul G. Singh. Port-of-Spain, Kingston: Longman Caribbean, 1972. 146p. bibliog.

This revised version of a doctoral thesis is one of the few books treating local government in Trinidad and Tobago. Singh traces the changes that the transplanted British idea of local government underwent in Jamaica, Barbados, Guyana and Trinidad up to 1968.

413 **Village-government relationships in Trinidad.**
Epeli Hanofa. In: *McGill studies in Caribbean anthropology.* Edited by Gerald Bentley, Frances Henry. Montreal: Centre for Developing Area Studies, McGill University, 1969, p. 6-18. (McGill University, Montreal. Centre for Developing Area Studies. Occasional Paper Series, no. 5).

The author finds communication between villages and the central government in Trinidad to be inadequate.

414 **Political leadership and administrative communication in new nation states; the case study of Trinidad and Tobago.**
Morton Kroll. *Social and Economic Studies*, vol. 16, no. 1 (March 1967), p. 17-33.

Kroll observed communication between upper level political leaders and career civil servants during the initial phase of Trinidad and Tobago's independence, from 1962 to 1963. In the case study that forms the basis of this article, he characterizes the types of communication that he perceived taking place between Trinidad's elected government and its administrative community.

Foreign Relations

General

415 **Leadership and foreign policy decision-making in a small state: Trinidad and Tobago's decision to enter the OAS.**
Basil A. Ince. In: *Issues in Caribbean international relations.* Edited by Basil A. Ince, Anthony T. Bryan, Herb Addo, Ramesh Ramsaran. St. Augustine, Trinidad: Institute of International Relations, University of the West Indies; Lanham, Maryland: University Press of America, 1983, p. 265-95.

An illuminating article that 'focuses on the decision-making process in the making of foreign policy in Trinidad and Tobago, with special emphasis on the leadership in that sphere of activity, and on a specific foreign policy decision, namely the entry of Trinidad and Tobago into the Organization of American States (OAS).' Ince concludes that Prime Minister Eric Williams played the dominant role in the government's decision to join the inter-hemispherical organization.

416 **Contemporary international relations of the Caribbean.**
Edited by Basil A. Ince. St. Augustine, Trinidad: Institute of International Relations, University of the West Indies, 1979. 359p. bibliog.

A recent collection of essays on Caribbean issues edited by the Director of the Institute of International Relations, University of the West Indies, St. Augustine, Trinidad. Dr. Ince has also held various portfolios in the cabinet of Trinidad and Tobago's current Prime Minister George Chambers. In a review of this book in the *Hispanic American Historic Review* vol. 60, no. 1 (Feb. 1980), p. 176, Wendell Bell called the volume 'must' reading for Caribbeanists.

417 **Perspectives from the Eastern tier: the foreign policies of Guyana, Trinidad and Tobago.**

Basil A. Ince. In: *The restless Caribbean; changing patterns of international relations.* Edited by Richard Millett, W. Marvin Will. New York: Praeger, 1979, p. 166-81. (Praeger Special Studies).

Ince contrasts the foreign policies of the two states during the Williams-Burnham era. Sections cover the two nations' relations with: the USA, Great Britain and the rest of Western Europe; the Communist world; Latin America in general; Venezuela; Brazil; Mexico; and the Caribbean region. Ince perceives a pattern in a decline in interest in regional integration in the area, with a corresponding increase in the pursuit of unilateral self-interest.

418 **The administration of foreign affairs in a very small developing country: the case of Trinidad and Tobago.**

Basil A. Ince. In: *Size, self-determination and international relations: the Caribbean.* Edited by Vaughan Lewis. Kingston: Institute of Social and Economic Research, University of the West Indies, 1976, p. 307-39.

One of the few articles available that deals with the foreign ministry and the diplomatic corps of a modern microstate.

419 **The racial factor in the international relations of Trinidad and Tobago.**

Basil A. Ince. *Caribbean Studies*, vol. 16, nos. 3-4 (Oct. 1976-Jan. 1977), p. 5-28.

The author of this article on the recent foreign relations of Trinidad states that 'studies which link race and international politics are rarities. . . . This article seeks to fill this gap in the growing literature of the international relations of [Trinidad and Tobago] because race cannot help being a factor in the international relations of racially-segmented states.'

420 **The media and foreign policy formation in small states; Trinidad and Tobago.**

Basil A. Ince. *International Journal*, vol. 31, no. 2 (Spring 1976), p. 270-92.

Ince examines the role played by newspapers, radio and television, and public opinion as expressed by these media in the formation of Trinidad's foreign policy. He finds the reporting of foreign news sparse, interest in world affairs limited, and input from the public lacking on the island. The article includes a synopsis of Trinidad's post-independence foreign policy, which Ince divides into two periods: independence to the 1970 February revolution and post-February revolution to the present (i.e., 1976). During the first period, Trinidad and Tobago were firmly aligned with the West; during the second, the country increased its dealings with the Eastern Bloc and the Third World and behaved as a non-aligned nation.

421 **Boundaries, possessions, and conflicts in Central and North America and the Caribbean.**
Gordon Ireland. Cambridge, Massachusetts: Harvard University Press, 1941. Reprinted, New York: Octagon, 1971. 432p. maps.

The dates of the possession of Tobago by various countries, 1498 to 1940, are given on p. 344-45.

422 **Boundaries, possessions, and conflicts in South America.**
Gordon Ireland. Cambridge, Massachusetts: Harvard University Press, 1938. Reprinted, New York: Octagon, 1971. 345p. maps.

Trinidad is covered on p. 271-73. Details and dates of the possession of the island by the Spanish, and later the British are provided and there is information on Trinidad and Britain's conflicts with Venezuela over the islands of Patos, Huevos, and Monos.

With African countries

423 **The Caribbean and Africa: a geo-political analysis.**
Linus A. Hoskins. In: *The Caribbean issues of emergence; socio-economic and political perspectives*. Edited by Vincent R. McDonald. Washington, DC: University Press of America, 1980, p. 147-69.

Hoskins examines the policies of Barbados, Guyana, Jamaica (under Manley), and Trinidad and Tobago with regard to Cuban involvement in Africa. Although these four countries have expressed their support for the liberation of Black Africans and all except Barbados have endorsed armed struggle, only Jamaica has specifically supported Cuban intervention in Africa.

With countries of the Caribbean region

424 **Regional diplomacy of the Commonwealth Caribbean.**
Neville Linton. *International Journal*, vol. 26, no. 2 (Spring 1971), p. 401-17.

A general discussion of post-Federation relations between the Caribbean states. Linton notes Trinidad and Tobago's key role as the leader in the development of cooperative foreign relations in the region. He also makes the point that although it has become characteristic of Commonwealth Caribbean diplomacy that emphasis is on direct dealings between prime ministers, this 'club' approach may prove inadequate in the future.

425 **The foreign relations of Jamaica and Trinidad and Tobago, 1960-65.**
Martin Ira Glassner. *Caribbean Studies*, vol. 10, no. 3 (Oct. 1970), p. 116-50. bibliog.

Considers the development of recent relations between Jamaica and Trinidad and Tobago, beginning with the launching of the West Indian Federation in January, 1958. The two nations clashed over their basic philosophies of what they wanted the Federation to be: Trinidad favoured a strong federation but with no freedom of movement between the islands; Jamaica wanted the opposite. Glassner contrasts Trinidad's and Jamaica's economic patterns and their foreign relations with the rest of the world. Tables comparing foreign trade and tourism statistics for the two countries and a list of their diplomatic missions abroad are appended to the article.

With Great Britain

426 **Europe in the Caribbean: the policies of Great Britain, France and the Netherlands toward their West Indian territories in the 20th century.**
Sir Harold Mitchell. Stanford, California: Hispanic American Society, Stanford University, 1963. 211p. maps. bibliog.

Studies the foreign policies of the colonial powers and their political and economic aims at the end of the colonial period. Of interest to Trinidadists are: Chapter three, 'The Caribbean policy of Great Britain from 1815 to 1939'; Chapter seven, 'Problems of closer union in the British Caribbean'; Chapter eight, 'The collapse of the West Indies Federation'; and Chapter nine, 'The Post-War British economic policy in the Caribbean.'

With Latin America

427 **National pursuits and regional definitions: the Caribbean as an interest area.**
Anthony P. Maingot. In: *Issues in Caribbean international relations.* Edited by Basil A. Ince, Anthony T. Bryan, Herb Addo, Ramesh Ramsaran. St. Augustine, Trinidad: Institute of International Relations, University of West Indies; Lanham, Maryland: University Press of America, 1983, p. 309-35. maps.

Analyses Trinidad's relations with Cuba and with Venezuela. The essay also discusses Venezuela's expanding interest in the Caribbean and the Trinidad-Venezuela fishing dispute.

428 **The twelve mile territorial sea: new focus for conflict in the Caribbean.**
Judith Ewell. *Caribbean Studies*, vol. 18, nos. 3-4 (Oct. 1978-Jan. 1979), p. 69-87.

This article includes a discussion of issues that are, or have been, areas of contention in the Gulf of Paria between Trinidad and its mainland neighbour Venezuela: fishing rights, division of the continental shelf, division of territorial waters, freedom of navigation, and ownership of three small islands in the Gulf (Huevos, Patos, and Monos).

429 **Conflict in Trinidad and Tobago's relations with Venezuela.**
H. S. Gill. In: *The Caribbean yearbook of international relations 1975.* Edited by L. F. Manigat. Leiden, The Netherlands: A. W. Sijthoff, 1976, p. 469-91.

Discusses the post-independence evolution of relations between Trinidad and Tobago and its mainland neighbour. Also of interest to Trinidadists is D. Boersner's 'The policy of Venezuela towards the Caribbean' in the same volume (p. 435-64).

430 **The relevance of Latin America to the foreign policy of Commonwealth Caribbean states.**
Roy Preiswerk. *Journal of Inter-American Studies*, vol. 11, no. 2 (April 1969), p. 245-71.

A clear presentation of the subject by the then Director of the Institute of International Relations, University of the West Indies, St. Augustine, Trinidad. Among the topics discussed relating to Trinidad are that nation's relations with Venezuela and the initiatives made by Trinidad towards the formation of an economic institution with Latin America. Preiswerk analyses the economic and political realities that account for Commonwealth Caribbean interest in Latin America as well as those that present obstacles to a rapprochement between the two regions.

Economy

431 **A note on the Trinidad and Tobago inflationary experience, 1965-1976.**
E. B. A. St. Cyr. *Social and Economic Studies*, vol. 28, no. 3 (Sept. 1979), p. 618-27. bibliog.

St. Cyr states that the proximate causes, in a macro-economic sense, of Trinidad and Tobago's inflation in recent years 'have been import prices, which acted as a trigger, money supply which served a permissive role at the very least, and expectations which reinforced the spiral.' According to his analysis, wages did not contribute actively to the inflation. St. Cyr also presented his research on the country's inflation in an earlier paper, *Rising prices: an exploratory theoretical and empirical study of Trinidad and Tobago* (Port-of-Spain: Central Statistical Office, 1974).

432 **The economics of water treatment: a Carribbean case study.**
Karl Theodore. *Social and Economic Studies*, vol. 28, no. 2 (June 1979), p. 364-96. bibliog.

An investigation of 'the nature of the costs involved in conventional water treatment [in order to] identify the underlying factors which make these costs greater or less.' The data upon which the study is based 'originates from one of the more developed water treatment systems in the Caribbean area – that of the Water and Sewerage Authority of Trinidad and Tobago.' The costs of this system are analysed for the years 1973 and 1974.

433 **Trinidad and Tobago's economic growth and the balance of trade: 1954-1968.**

W. Joefield-Napier. *Social and Economic Studies*, vol. 27, no. 4 (Dec. 1978), p. 375-402. bibliog.

A theoretical analysis of the relationship between economic growth and the balance of payments in 'a developing economy which exhibited a highly skewed pattern of growth in the post-war years, namely, Trinidad and Tobago.' The author tests Hicks' hypothesis that enhanced productivity can only lead to an adverse balance of trade situation, if and only if, a country's economic growth has been uniform, as it relates to Trinidad's economic growth and balance of trade and finds the hypothesis invalid.

434 **An econometric model of Trinidad and Tobago 1960-1971.**

Unanan Persad. *Social and Economic Studies*, vol. 24, no. 4 (Dec. 1975), p. 389-410. bibliog.

'Based on time series annual observations, [this article] provides a macro-economic structural description of [Trinidad's] economy with statistically estimated quantitative parameters.'

435 **East Indians in the economy of Trinidad and Tobago.**

Winston Dookeran. In: *Calcutta to Caroni: the East Indians of Trinidad.* Edited by John Gaffar La Guerre. Port-of-Spain: Longmans Caribbean, 1974, p. 69-83.

Dookeran demonstrates that the East Indians are economically the least privileged group in Trinidadian society.

436 **The mechanics of independence; patterns of political and economic transformation in Trinidad and Tobago.**

A. N. R. Robinson. Cambridge, Massachusetts: MIT Press, 1971. 200p. bibliog.

This volume links economic conditions with political change and is 'intended to contribute to an understanding of the problems not only of Trinidad and Tobago and the Caribbean but also of ex-colonial countries in general.' After four chapters dealing with Trinidad's colonial past and one chapter on the short-lived Federation of the West Indies, Robinson describes and discusses adjustments made to the Trinidadian economic system in order to realign the economy from a colonial to an independent focus. Separate chapters cover reforms made on tariffs and indirect taxes, banking, insurance, direct taxes, and the budget. An appendix includes political documents which are important in the history of Trinidad and Tobago: the Cedula of Colonization of 1783; Council Paper no. 177 (which united Tobago with Trinidad); and the Independence Constitution of 1962.

437 **A step towards a political economy of development (illustrated by the case of Trinidad/Tobago).**
Dudley Seers. *Social and Economic Studies*, vol. 18, no. 3 (Sept. 1969), p. 217-53.

This lengthy and important article on the political economy of developing countries uses Trinidad and Tobago as its chief example. Seers states that he chose Trinidad as his illustration because 'in Trinidad more than 10 per cent of the labour force are out of work. . . . If there is one generalization that can safely be made about the whole of Africa, Asia and Latin America, it is that . . . unemployment . . . has become massive, chronic and dangerous.' Besides discussing employment policy in Trinidad, Seers sketches 'A scenario for a viable Trinidadian economy in the 1980's' and suggests changes that he feels should be made in the island's economy.

438 **Wage-policy issues in an underdeveloped economy: Trinidad and Tobago.**
Havelock Brewster. Mona, Jamaica: Institute of Social and Economic Research, University of the West Indies, 1969. 101p.

Studies economic policy in relation to labour issues in the 1950s and 1960s.

439 **An evaluation of incentive legislation in Trinidad and Tobago.**
Eric Armstrong. Mona, Jamaica: Institute of Social and Economic Research, University of the West Indies, 1967. 32p. (Studies in Regional Economic Integration, vol. 2, no. 5: Import Substitution in Jamaica and Trinidad and Tobago; part A: Incentive Legislation in Trinidad and Tobago).

A look at the government's policy of promoting industrial development in Trinidad and Tobago which, the author comments, 'appears to have been conceived quite haphazardly without any clear idea of the long-term aims to be achieved by such a policy.' Thus, Armstrong's purpose in this study is 'to show what effects incentive legislation, subsidies, etc. have had on employment, production, earnings of foreign exchange, and the reduction of imports.'

440 **Some steps towards an optimal foodstuffs consumption, production and importation programme for Trinidad and Tobago.**
S. DeCastro, John Lauritz. *Social and Economic Studies*, vol. 16, no. 4 (Dec. 1967), p. 349-64.

The authors state that their paper 'is an account of some preliminary steps towards the construction of a mathematical model which represents with some degree of realism the food sub-sector of the economy of Trinidad and Tobago. Using linear programming (l.p.) as the basic mathematical formulation, we hope to find that consumption, production and importation programme for food items which will minimize the total cost of fulfilling the nutritional and palatability requirements of the nation.'

441 **Distribution of income in Trinidad and Tobago and comparison with distribution of income in Jamaica.**
E. Ahiram. *Social and Economic Studies*, vol. 15, no. 2 (June 1966), p. 103-20.

'The main objective of this paper is to present and analyse a fairly comprehensive and reliable set of data on personal income distribution in Trinidad and to compare these findings with those for Jamaica.' The study is organized in three sections: the first deals with distribution of income in households in Trinidad-Tobago; the second covers inequality of incomes between industrial sectors; and section three studies changes in inequalities of income.

442 **Growth and structural change in the economy of Trinidad and Tobago, 1951-1961.**
Frank B. Rampersad. Mona, Jamaica: Institute of Social and Economic Research, University of the West Indies, 1963. 95p.

An in-depth analysis, much of it presented in tabular form, of the economic growth and changes in the structure of Trinidad's economy in the decade that preceded independence. The author was Senior Economist in the Central Statistical Office of Trinidad and Tobago.

443 **Projections of the growth of the economy of Trinidad and Tobago.**
Eric Armstrong. *Social and Economic Studies*, vol. 12, no. 3 (Sept. 1963), p. 283-306.

Presents projections of the growth rate of Trinidad's Gross Domestic Product (GDP), for the years 1959 to 1975. Armstrong considers each sector of the nation's economy.

444 **Quarterly Economic Report.**
Port-of-Spain: Central Statistical Office, 1950- . quarterly.

Publishes statistics collected in the Economic Indicators section of the Central Statistical Office.

Investment, Finance and Banking

445 **Notes on financial changes in Trinidad and Tobago, 1966-1978.**
Compton Bourne. *Social and Economic Studies*, vol. 31, no. 4 (Dec. 1982), p. 171-91. bibliog.

Highlights financial developments in Trinidad and Tobago during the oil boom of the second half of the 1970s. The structure of Trinidad's financial system, post-1974, is compared and contrasted with that of the pre-1974 period. Includes tables.

446 **The multinational corporations, external control and the problem of development: the case of Trinidad and Tobago.**
Ken I. Boodhoo. In: *The restless Caribbean; changing patterns of international relations.* Edited by Richard Millett, W. Marvin Will. New York: Praeger, 1979, p. 62-70. (Praeger Special Studies).

The author analyses 'the implications of MNC activity for the development process with respect to the Caribbean, by examining MNC activity and attempted state control in Trinidad and Tobago.' Boodhoo concentrates on the petroleum industry, which dominates Trinidad's economy, and the sugar industry, which is the largest private employer of labour in the country. He points out that the goals of foreign investment of the multinational corporations (MNCs), particularly profit maximization, may conflict with the development objectives of the government and the electorate.

447 **Public finance in Trinidad and Tobago.**
Patrick Baptiste. *Social and Economic Studies*, vol. 26, no. 4 (Dec. 1977), p. 477-500.

An examination of the fiscal management of the Trinidad and Tobago economy for the period 1964 to 1975. The text is supplemented by tables covering that decade's index of retail prices; monetary base, bank credit and money supply;

central government revenue; central government expenditure; capital expenditure; central government fiscal operations; central government public debt; and public debt and debt servicing.

448 **Central Bank of Trinidad and Tobago Monthly Statistical Digest.**
Port-of-Spain: Central Bank of Trinidad and Tobago, 1968- . monthly.

Provides statistics on Trinidad and Tobago's finance and banking.

Business, Trade and Industry

General

449 **Technology leasing as the latest imperialist phase: a case study of Guyana and Trinidad.**
Maurice A. Odle. *Social and Economic Studies*, vol. 1, no. 1 (March 1979), p. 189-233.

The author states that 'technology leasing in the English-speaking Caribbean fits very much into the general framework of dependent underdevelopment.' His paper examines contractual arrangements in regard to technology leasing, with particular reference to manufacturing enterprises, the patent structure, the impact of the leasing process on government objectives, and the alternatives to technology leasing facing developing nations. Data drawn from Trinidad and Guyana are used to exemplify the author's points.

450 **Multinational corporations and black power.**
Harry G. Matthews. Cambridge, Massachusetts: Schenkman, 1976. 124p. bibliog.

Studies the social aspects of expatriate-controlled international business enterprises in Barbados and Trinidad, centring on the conflict between the aims of multinational corporations and Black nationalist aspirations.

451 **Tourism and development; a case study of the Commonwealth Caribbean.**
John M. Bryden. Cambridge, England: Cambridge University Press, 1973. 236p. bibliog.

Based on the author's thesis at the University of East Anglia, this volume is a case study of the tourist trade in the former British colonies of the Caribbean.

452 **The feasibility of caustic soda/chlorine production in Trinidad and Tobago.**

Steve De Castro, Monty Dolly. *Social and Economic Studies*, vol. 21, no. 4 (Dec. 1972), p. 404-61. bibliog.

An investigation of the economic and technical feasibility of producing caustic soda in one Caribbean territory, Trinidad and Tobago, in order to provide the substance to the bauxite companies of Jamaica and Guyana for use in processing their ores into alumina. Currently, most caustic is imported from the United States. The authors conclude that the chemical could be produced cheaply enough in Trinidad and Tobago to compete with caustic produced outside the region.

453 **Readings in the political economy of the Caribbean; a collection of reprints of articles on Caribbean political economy with suggested further reading.**

Edited by Norman Girvan, Owen Jefferson. Kingston: New World Group, 1971. 287p.

Contains E. Carrington's essay 'Industrialisation by invitation in Trinidad and Tobago since 1950.'

454 **The influence of culture on business in pluralistic society: a study of Trinidad, West Indies.**

Tony H. Bonaparte. *American Journal of Economics and Sociology*, vol. 28, no. 3 (July 1969), p. 285-300.

Bonaparte characterizes Trinidad as a plural society and analyses the impact of one variable – culture – on business on the island. Based on data collected in the 1960s, the article discusses the cultural setting; Creole culture and British influences; attitudes towards work, management, and authority; the forms of organization found in Trinidadian business; and inter-racial groups. From his analysis, Bonaparte draws some interesting conclusions: for example, that the Trinidadian manager does not operate exclusively to maximize profits.

455 **Some aspects of the external trade and payments of Trinidad and Tobago, 1951-1959.**

Frank B. Rampersad. *Social and Economic Studies*, vol. 12, no. 2 (June 1963), p. 101-40.

Examines certain characteristics of Trinidad and Tobago's external trade and payments in relation to the general economic circumstances of the period 1951 to 1959.

456 **Overseas Trade: Annual Report.**

Port-of-Spain: Central Statistical Office, 1951- . annual.

A summary of the year's foreign trade, issued in three parts, A, B, and C.

Oil industry

457 **In whose interest? nationalization and bargaining with the petroleum multinationals: the Trinidad and Tobago experience.**
Trevor M. A. Farrell. In: *Issues in Caribbean international relations*. Edited by Basil A. Ince, Anthony T. Bryan, Herb Addo, Ramesh Ramsaran. St. Augustine, Trinidad: Institute of International Relations, University of the West Indies; Lanham, Maryland: University Press of America, 1983, p. 171-208.

Presents two case studies, based on Trinidad and Tobago's recent experience in oil nationalization. The first concerns the 1969 purchase of the BP Oil Company and the formation of a joint venture company, Trinidad-Tesoro, with an American oil company, Tesoro of Texas. The second looks at the 1974 nationalization of Shell Trinidad Ltd. Farrell concludes that '. . . multinational corporations have increasingly learnt to make nationalization and joint ventures work for them.'

458 **A tale of two issues; nationalization, the transfer of technology and the petroleum multinationals in Trinidad and Tobago.**
Trevor M. A. Farrell. *Social and Economic Studies*, vol. 28, no. 1 (March 1979), p. 234-81.

Farrell draws on Trinidad's two generations of experience with multinational corporations in the petroleum industry to conclude that there is nothing automatic about the transfer of technology by the MNCs to the underdeveloped countries in which they operate. He also concludes that 'there is serious question about the value of some of what has been called nationalization in underdeveloped countries in recent years.' Farrell dealt with the same topic in his earlier paper, *The multinational corporations, the transfer of technology, and the human resources problem in the Trinidad and Tobago petroleum industry* (Mona, Jamaica: Institute for Social and Economic Research, University of the West Indies, 1977).

459 **The oil industry in the economy of Trinidad.**
Vernon C. Mulchansingh. *Caribbean Studies*, vol. 11, no. 1 (April 1971), p. 73-100.

After a sketch of the history of the petroleum industry in Trinidad, Mulchansingh explains its significant contribution to the country's economic life as of the late 1960s. Charts and tables supplement the text.

Manpower and Employment

460 **Unemployment and social life; a sociological study of the unemployed in Trinidad.**
Farley Brathwaite. Bridgetown: Antilles Publications, 1983. 165p. bibliog.

Based on the author's doctoral thesis for the University of Pittsburgh, 1979, this is a pioneering study of the consequences, as opposed to the causes, of unemployment. Unemployed Trinidadians were interviewed in order to 'identify, describe and discuss certain aspects of social life among the unemployed'; 'show how these aspects of social life . . . varied according to socio-demographic factors'; and 'explore the theoretical significance of the findings, [especially in regard to] the relevance of the subjective factor.'

461 **A comment on 'The measurement of unemployment.'**
Ralph M. Henry. *Social and Economic Studies*, vol. 29, nos. 2-3 (July-Sept. 1980), p. 52-55. bibliog.

Henry reviews Trevor M. A. Farrell's 'The measurement of unemployment and the labour force in Trinidad and Tobago: are the official figures wrong?' (q.v.), and calls for more studies of the same type.

462 **The measurement of unemployment and the labour force in Trinidad and Tobago: are the official figures wrong?**
Trevor M. A. Farrell. *Social and Economic Studies*, vol. 29, nos. 2-3 (June-Sept. 1980), p. 35-51.

This study by an economist 'attempts to test the reliability of the labour-force statistics provided for Trinidad and Tobago.' Farrell discusses the types of error which are possible and defines the concepts used in the government's labour-force statistics. He then checks the consistency of the statistics and points out a discrepancy in the official unemployment figures.

463 **The unemployment crisis in Trinidad and Tobago: its current dimensions and some projections to 1985.**
Trevor M. A. Farrell. *Social and Economic Studies*, vol. 27, no. 2 (June 1978), p. 117-52. bibliog.

A detailed study of unemployment in Trinidad and Tobago, which Farrell terms 'a significant socio-economic problem.'

464 **Report of the Mission on short-term action to combat unemployment in Trinidad and Tobago, November 29-December 15, 1971.**
Organization of American States. Washington, DC: General Secretariat of the Organization of American States, 1974. 83p.

A report on unemployment in Trinidad and Tobago in 1971, originally presented to the Chairman of the Inter-American Committee on the Alliance for Progress.

465 **Employment in Trinidad and Tobago.**
Sidney Chernick (et al.). Washington, DC: International Bank for Reconstruction and Development, 1973. 2 vols. in 1. map.

A World Bank country report, based on the findings of an economic mission led by Sidney Chernick which visited Trinidad and Tobago in April and May 1972.

466 **The adjustment of displaced workers in a labour-surplus economy: a case study of Trinidad and Tobago.**
Roy Darrow Thomas. Mona, Jamaica: Institute for Social and Economic Research, University of the West Indies, 1972. 118p. bibliog.

A study of workers laid off because of technological advances in the petroleum mining and refining industry. Based on the author's doctoral dissertation, Cornell University, 1969.

467 **Changes in the demand for and the supply of labour in the Commonwealth Caribbean, 1946-1960.**
J. Harewood. *Social and Economic Studies*, vol. 21, no. 1 (March 1972), p. 44-60. bibliog.

An economic study of the British Caribbean area, focusing primarily on the changing manpower supply in Barbados and Trinidad and Tobago. Harewood is also the author of a research paper, *A comparison of labour force data in Trinidad and Tobago, 1946-64* (Port-of-Spain: Central Statistical Office, 1965).

468 **The growth of employment under export-biassed underdevelopment: Trinidad.**

Havelock Brewster. *Social and Economic Studies*, vol. 21, no. 2 (June 1972), p. 153-69. bibliog.

'This paper, after commenting briefly on some current theories [of the growth of unemployment in less-developed countries], will present the results and some of the implications of an exercise which relates data on changes in the volume of employment to changes in a number of other economic variables for Trinidad, a country with a high level of dependence on exports of petroleum and sugar.'

Labour and Trade Unions

469 **An introduction to the life and times of T. U. B. Butler, the father of the nation.**
Nyahuma Obika. Point Fortin, Trinidad: Caribbean Historical Society, 1983. 219p. bibliog.

A partisan account of the political career of Tubal Uriah 'Buzz' Butler (1897-1970), trade unionist and working class political leader in Trinidad in the 1930s.

470 **The political uses of commissions of enquiry (1): the imperial-colonial West Indies context; the Forster and Moyne Commissions.**
Howard Johnson. *Social and Economic Studies*, vol. 27, no. 3 (Sept. 1978), p. 256-63. bibliog.

This enlightening article examines how the British Colonial Office used commissions of enquiry to calm unrest in the West Indies. The Forster Commission was appointed in response to the riots in Trinidad's oilfields in 1937, which the Colonial Office conceptualized as a labour problem. The Commission was empowered to both investigate conditions in Trinidad and to make recommendations. The article also deals with the Royal Commission to the West Indies headed by Lord Moyne. The bibliography includes printed materials and British government documents relating to the commissions.

471 **Notes and comments: towards industrial democracy in Trinidad.**
S. Rambachan. *Social and Economic Studies*, vol. 26, no. 2 (June 1977), p. 234-38.

A brief discussion of attempts to democratize the workplace in Trinidad through worker participation and the humanization of working life.

472 **The politics of protest in Trinidad; the strikes and disturbances of 1937.**

W. Richard Jacobs. *Caribbean Studies*, vol. 17, nos. 1-2 (April-July 1977), p. 5-54.

A solid and detailed presentation of an important event in Trinidad's labour history. Jacobs states that his aim is 'to try to establish what exactly did happen in 1937, why it happened, and what factors influenced the direction of events.' He begins with a summary of the socio-political situation in Trinidad in the 1930s: the system of crown colony government, the economy, and the main areas of economic activity – oil, sugar, and cocoa. He then sketches the religious milieu and the individuals and groups involved in the strike: Arthur Cipriani and the Trinidad Workingmen's Association; Butler and the British Empire Workers and Citizens' Home Rule Party; Adrian Cola Rienzi and the Trinidad Citizens' League; the Black welfare, cultural and social associations; the Toussaint L'Ouverture Club; and the Legislative Council members who supported the strikes. He goes on to cover the strikers and their demands in the various industries involved and describes the disturbances themselves, noting the techniques used by the workers to mobilize, the organization of the workers, and the factors that influenced the direction of the strike. The article ends with a general discussion of the implications of the resolution of the strikes for Trinidadian society as a whole.

473 **History of the working class in the 20th century (Trinidad and Tobago).**

Bukka Rennie. Port-of-Spain, New York, London, Toronto: New Beginning Movement, 1973. 167p.

Reviewed in the *Pan-African Journal*, vol. 8, no. 2 (Summer 1975), p. 237-41, by 'T.S.' who describes the work as 'the history of working class self-activity and self-organization in Trinidad from 1919 to 1956 . . . told from the perspective of the activist rather than the scholar.' 'T.S.' feels that Rennie's book restores the Negro Welfare Association of the 1930s and 1940s to its rightful place in Trinidad's labour history.

474 **Members for Trinidad.**

Bary Simpson-Halley. *Journal of Caribbean History*, vol. 6 (May 1973), p. 81-93.

Concerns relations between the British Labour Party and Labour political leaders and the Trinidad Workingmen's Association from 1906 on. Two Labour MPs, Thomas Summerbell and Joseph Pointer, served as liaison between the TWA and the British Labour Party and tried to look after Trinidadian labour's interest in the British Parliament.

475 **The Trinidad Workingmen's Association and the origins of popular protest in a crown colony.**

Brinsley Samaroo. *Social and Economic Studies*, vol. 21, no. 2 (June 1972), p. 205-22. bibliog.

'This paper seeks to trace the growth of one [militant workers' pressure] group in Trinidad, the Workingmen's Association (WMA) and to examine the role which it played in the struggle for an amelioration of [working and political] conditions [in Trinidad] from the date of its inception in 1897 to around 1920,' when Captain Cipriani joined the group just after the First World War.

Transport

476 **A model approach to the understanding of the transportation network in Trinidad, W.I.**

Vernon C. Mulchansingh. *Caribbean Quarterly*, vol. 16, no. 3 (Sept. 1970), p. 23-51. maps. bibliog.

Mulchansingh shows how in Trinidad the transportation system has developed 'mainly in relation to the agricultural (sugar cane and cocoa) and petroleum sectors [of the overall economy].' This geographical transportation study should also be of interest to historians, as the author provides a valuable summary of the growth of the transport network from early times. The text is enhanced with maps, tables, and charts.

Agriculture and Rural Conditions

477 **The changing fortunes of a Trinidad peasantry: a case study.**
David Harrison. In: *Peasants, plantations and rural communities in the Caribbean.* Edited by Malcolm Cross, Arnaud Marks. Guildford, England: Dept. of Sociology of the University of Surrey and the Dept. of Caribbean Studies of the Royal Institute of Linguistics and Anthropology, Leiden, Netherlands, 1979, p. 54-85.

Harrison traces the agricultural community of Demsay, near Toco in northeastern Trinidad, through a century (1860-1972) of change.

478 **Dairying and development at Wallerfield, Trinidad.**
H. J. Pollard, D. A. Eastwood. *Tijdschrift voor Economische en Sociale Geographie*, vol. 67, no. 5 (1976), p. 289-99.

A study of an agricultural development project. Trinidad's dairy industry was also a subject of a study by Ali Ridwan, *Land settlement planning in Trinidad and Tobago: a study of the dairy and pig industry* (Mona, Jamaica: Institute of Social and Economic Research, University of the West Indies, 1974).

479 **Plantation infrastructure and labor mobility in Guyana and Trinidad.**
Bonham C. Richardson. In: *Migration and development; implications for ethnic identity and political conflict.* Edited by Helen I. Safa, Brian M. DuToit. Paris, The Hague: Mouton, 1975. p. 205-06. bibliog. (World Anthropology).

Based on field research in Guyana in 1967 and 1968-1969, and in Trinidad in the summer of 1971. Richardson challenges the view that ethnic identity explains rural livelihood behaviour in these two countries. Rather, he believes that the plantation experience is the crucial factor behind both the historical and the contemporary economic behaviour of small-scale rural inhabitants in both territories.

480 **The origins and early development of cane farming in Trinidad, 1882-1906.**
Howard Johnson. *Journal of Caribbean History*, vol. 5 (Nov. 1972), p. 46-74.
'Cane farming [is] a system by which cultivators grow sugar cane without owning mills to grind it. [This system] developed in Trinidad in the late 19th century.' This paper is the first attempt to study the cane-farming system in itself. Howard's paper examines the development of cane farming from 1882 to 1906, and discusses the establishment, organization, support, popularity, and problems of the system during a twenty-five year period.

481 **The development of small-scale farming: two cases from the Commonwealth Caribbean.**
D. T. Edwards. *Caribbean Quarterly*, vol. 18, no. 1 (March 1972), p. 59-71. bibliog.
Contrasts peasant farming in Jamaica in the 1950s with small-scale vegetable production in Aranjuez, Trinidad.

482 **Aranjuez: a case study in rural development.**
Andrew MacMillan. *Journal of Administration Overseas*, vol. 9, no. 2 (April 1970), p. 84-95.
An account of a small, successful market gardening enterprise at Aranjuez, Trinidad, which makes the point that 'where government agencies are suspected of being politically motivated, their effectiveness will be severely limited. The solution suggested is that technical assistance might best be handled objectively by a non-government institution such as a university.' The article also includes a brief history of the area and a discussion of how its economic growth was achieved.

483 **Agriculture in the development of Trinidad and Tobago; a comment.**
G. L. F. Beckford. *Social and Economic Studies*, vol. 14, no. 2 (June 1965), p. 217-20.
A brief discussion of the programme for agricultural development outlined in the Trinidad and Tobago Draft Second Five-Year Plan, 1964-68. Beckford notes that expansion of agricultural output is crucial for Trinidadian development.

484 **Projection of cocoa output in Grenada, Trinidad and Jamaica, 1960-75.**
Clive Y. Thomas. *Social and Economic Studies*, vol. 13, no. 1 (March 1964), p. 94-117.
'An attempt to estimate the long-term supply position of cocoa in the major West Indian producing areas.' The section on Trinidad (p. 102-07), covers the

organization of the cocoa industry, processing, and marketing as well as projections for output. Tables.

485 **Rice in the British Caribbean islands and British Guyana, 1950-1975.**

A. Kunda. *Social and Economic Studies*, vol. 13, no. 2 (June 1964), p. 243-81.

Provides a short description of Trinidad's rice industry, covers supply and demand of rice from 1950 to 1960, and projects trends in the demand and supply of the Trinidadian commodity for the years 1961 to 1975.

486 **Toward an operational definition of community.**

Morris Freilich. *Rural Sociology*, vol. 28, no. 2 (June 1963), p. 117-27.

'An attempt is made in this paper to provide certain operationally defined criteria for community.' Freilich uses as his data the interactions of the inhabitants of the Trinidadian village of Anamat. The result is an interesting picture of the communication patterns of Trinidad's rural villagers.

487 **The plantation: a bibliography.**

Edgar T. Thompson. Washington, DC: Social Science Section, Dept. of Cultural Affairs, Pan American Union, 1957. 98p. (Social Science Monographs, no. 4).

An unannotated list of 1,347 items, including both monographs and journal articles, on the worldwide phenomenon of the plantation: its definition, description, theory, natural history, agriculture, geography, and ecology. Both factual and fictional materials dealing with this type of agricultural organization are included. Materials on the West Indies are listed on p. 62-67.

Statistics

488 **National primary socio-economic data structures IX: Barbados, Jamaica, Trinidad and Tobago.**
J. E. Greene, Reive Robb. *International Social Science Journal*, vol. 33, no. 2 (1981), p. 339-414. bibliog.

An excellent presentation of information sources – public, institutional, and private – where statistical socio-economic data on the three nations of the title can be found. The article covers the history of the British Caribbean's censuses, notes labour-force data collection, and surveys the organization and the functions of the statistical services in the three countries. A chart of the organization of the Trinidad and Tobago Central Statistical Office is provided. The article also reviews the work of the social research centre at the University of the West Indies. The authors mention the problems that dog the region's efforts to coordinate, maintain, and upgrade statistical services.

489 **Statistical activities of the American nations: Trinidad and Tobago.**
Inter-American Statistical Institute. Washington, DC: General Secretariat, Organization of American States, 1979. 75p.

This booklet was prepared for publication by the Central Statistical Office of Trinidad and Tobago, under the direction of Leo C. Pujades, Director of Statistics. After a section describing the historical development of the Central Statistical Office, the volume presents the organization, activities, and services of the government bureau in the 1970s.

490 **Annual Statistical Digest.**
Port-of-Spain: Central Statistical Office, 1952- . annual.

A compendium of social and economic statistics furnished by the various sections of the Central Statistical Office. There is usually a two to three year delay in its publication.

Education

491 **White Paper on National Institute of Higher Education (research, science and technology), Republic of Trinidad and Tobago.**
Introduction by Selwyn D. Ryan. *Caribbean Studies*, vol. 17, nos. 3-4 (Oct. 1977-Jan. 1978), p. 183-231.

The *White Paper* issued by the Government Printery of the Republic of Trinidad and Tobago on 17 October 1977, is reproduced in full, on p. 194-231, preceded by Ryan's ten page introduction. The *White Paper* states the government's proposed policy on scientific and technological education and research in Trinidad and Tobago and on the restructuring of the University of the West Indies. Ryan criticizes the proposal's possible deleterious effect on the autonomy and integrity of the university.

492 **The establishment of Queen's Collegiate School in Trinidad, 1857-1867.**
C. Campbell. *Caribbean Journal of Education*, vol. 2, no. 2 (Dec. 1975), p. 71-86.

An early history of the government-run college, modeled on the British public school, that offered a secular and classical education to Trinidadians. Queen's Collegiate School was the predecessor of Queen's Royal College, which counts among its alumni such distinguished Trinidadians as C. L. R. James, Eric Williams, and V. S. Naipaul.

493 **Educational planning in Trinidad and Tobago.**
Michael Alleyne. *Caribbean Studies*, vol. 11, no. 4 (Jan. 1972), p. 73-81.

This article looks at education in Trinidad and Tobago in the light of the nation's commitment to planning, both in education and in its total development. Alleyne notes that the economic value of education has been stressed in developing countries such as Trinidad.

494 **The effect of the home on the school in Trinidad.**
P. B. Dyer. *Social and Economic Studies*, vol. 17, no. 4 (Dec. 1968), p. 435-41.

This study of the effects of home environment on the achievement of elementary pupils in Trinidad's schools is based on the author's doctoral dissertation. Dyer infers from an analysis of data collected in Trinidad 'that it is not so much what the parent has as what he does with and for the child that has the greater influence on the child's school performance.'

495 **Problems to be faced in the use of English as the medium of education in four West Indian territories.**
Robert B. LePage. In: *Language problems in developing nations.* Edited by Joshua A. Fishman, Charles A. Ferguson, Jyotirindra Das Gupta. New York: Wiley, 1968, p. 431-42.

LePage directed the Lingusitic Survey of the British West Indies from 1950 to 1960. In this brief paper, he characterizes the language problems besetting the educational systems of Jamaica, British Honduras, Guyana, and Trinidad and Tobago, and relates these problems to the social and psychological situation obtaining in these former British colonies. He goes on to make some suggestions for changes in teacher training to meet the needs and challenges of independence.

496 **Reports and repercussions in West Indian education, 1835-1933.**
Shirley C. Gordon. London: Ginn, 1968. 190p.

Gordon presents and discusses eight historical documents on West Indian education. She notes in her foreword to the volume that the reports she has collected are all 'official, [and in] all but one case . . . are the work of a commission to enquire into a special problem of the government of the time . . . they reveal the attitudes of the colonial administrations, supervised by the Colonial Office, in providing education for the West Indian colonies.' The volume is divided into three sections: 'The reports and the reporters'; 'The main topics of the reports'; and 'Extracts from the reports.' Documents dealing with education in Trinidad are: the *Keenan Report* (1869), the *Education Commission Report* (1916), and the *Marriott-Mayhew Report* (1931-32). This material also appeared serially in issues of the *Caribbean Quarterly* between September, 1962, and December, 1964.

497 **A note on school enrolment in Trinidad and Tobago, 1960.**
G. W. Roberts. *Social and Economic Studies*, vol. 16, no. 2 (June 1967), p. 113-23.

An analysis of the school population of Trinidad and Tobago as a stationary system, using data derived from the 1960 population census.

498 **Documents which have guided education and policy in the West Indies: Education Commission Report, Trinidad, 1916.**
Shirley C. Gordon. *Caribbean Quarterly*, vol. 10, no. 2 (June 1964), p. 19-39.

The Education Commission Report of 1916 initiated a beneficial change in Trinidad's education by changing the administrative machinery and initiating a new approach to elementary education. This article quotes extensively from the report.

499 **Documents which have guided educational policy in the West Indies no. 8: Report of the Commissioners Mayhew and Marriott on secondary and primary education in Trinidad, Barbados, Leeward Islands and Windward Islands, 1931-32.**
Shirley C. Gordon. *Caribbean Quarterly*, vol. 10, no. 4 (Dec. 1964), p. 3-32.

'This commission resulted from an offer by the Colonial Office to send a member of the Advisory Committee on Education in the Colonies to examine educational problems in association with one of the education officers serving in the West Indies. Arthur Mayhew, who had had a long career in India, came from London and F. C. Marriott, Director of Education for Trinidad, was his colleague.'

Languages

Yoruba

500 **Trinidad Yoruba – notes on survivals.**
Maureen Warner. *Caribbean Quarterly*, vol. 17, no. 2 (June 1971), p. 40-49.

Warner describes the variety of Yoruba spoken by two native Trinidadians (an octogenarian and a nonagenarian) who had learned the language from their elders as children in Trinidad.

English

501 **The African impact of language and literature in the English-speaking Caribbean.**
Maureen Warner Lewis. In: *Africa and the Caribbean; the legacies of a link.* Edited by Margaret E. Crahan, Franklin W. Knight. Baltimore, Maryland; London: Johns Hopkins University Press, 1979, p. 101-23.

Sociolinguist Lewis begins her article with a heavily documented case study of the influence of African language in Trinidad, providing a list of Yoruba idiomatic expressions that can be paralleled in Trinidadian Creole English. She also points out that Yoruba continues to exist as a spoken language on the island. The article ends with a discussion of Caribbean Anglophone writers' use of stylistic literary devices and genres of African origin.

502 **Creole languages and national identity in the Caribbean.**
Keith Q. Warner. *CLA Journal*, vol. 20, no. 3 (March 1977), p. 319-32.

This general article on both French-based and English-based Creole languages in the Caribbean area includes references to some of the problems and conflicts occurring between standard English and Creole English in Trinidad.

503 **'Creole' culture and language in Trinidad: a socio-historical sketch.**
Donald Winford. *Caribbean Studies*, vol. 15, no. 3 (Oct. 1975), p. 31-56. bibliog.

Winford emphasizes the role played by the use of English in the process of assimilation and acculturation that took place among the various immigrant groups in Trinidad in the 19th century. His article includes sections on the spread of English from 1797 to 1900; influences of foreign languages on Trinidadian English; social factors involved in the spread of English; the decline of [French] patois; and the language situation in Trinidad today.

504 **Trinidad English – the origin of 'mamaguy' and 'picong.'**
Kemlin Laurence. *Caribbean Quarterly*, vol. 17, no. 2 (June 1971), p. 36-39.

'Mamaguy,' a verb meaning 'to tease, especially by flattery,' and 'picong,' a noun that means 'ribbing or teasing,' are two Hispanicisms that have wide currency and popularity at all levels of Trinidadian English. Laurence explains the derivation and usage of these terms.

505 **Trinidadian folk usage and standard English: a contrastive study.**
Henry J. Richards. *Word*, vol. 26, no. 1 (April 1970), p. 79-87.

Richards contrasts the syntactical structures of Trinidad Creole English or 'folk speech' and standard English, finding essential grammatical differences between the two idioms.

506 **Some Spanish words in the English-based dialect of Trinidad.**
Henry J. Richards. *Hispania*, vol. 53, no. 2 (May 1970), p. 263-66.

Richards discusses several Trinidadian English words that have evolved from Spanish.

507 **Some vestiges of Spanish in the dialect of Trinidad.**
Henry Richards. *Hispania*, vol. 49, no. 3 (Sept. 1966), p. 481-83.

Richards identifies a number of words current in colloquial Trinidadian English as derived from Spanish. He discusses how the Trinidadian form of the words evolved, and notes how some words have changed their grammatical function as well as their pronunciation.

508 **Trinibagianese; words and phrases, old and new, peculiar to the speech of Trinidadians and Tobagonians.**
C. R. Ottley. Diego Martin, Trinidad?: n.p., 1966. 2 vols. 2nd ed. (Little Books on Trinidad and Tobago, nos. 1-2).

This set of pamphlets glosses words found in Trinidad's and Tobago's Creole English dialects. Volume one was first published separately as *Trinidadianese; how to old talk in Trinidad* (Diego Martin, Trinidad: Granderson, 1965).

509 **Prestamos linguisticos en tres idiomas trinitarios.** (Loan-words in three Trinidadian languages.)
Robert Wallace Thompson. *Estudios Americanos*, vol. 12, no. 61 (Oct. 1956), p. 249-54.

The three languages referred to in the title of this article are Spanish, French Creole, and Trinidadian English. The author discusses the lexical interactions that took place between these languages in Trinidad, and lists borrowings found in all three languages. The text of the article is in Spanish.

French Creole

510 **On the phonemics of the French Creole of Trinidad.**
Morris F. Goodman. *Word*, vol. 14, nos. 2-3 (Aug.-Dec. 1958), p. 208-12.

A linguistic description of the segmental phonemes of Trinidad French Creole which identifies thirty phonemes. This is one of the few articles that deals with Trinidad's French patois.

511 **The theory and practice of Creole grammar.**
J. J. Thomas. Port-of-Spain: Chronicle Publishing Office, 1869. Reprinted, London: New Beacon, 1969. 135p. bibliog.

The earliest work on Trinidad's French Creole dialect. The facsimile reprint has an introduction by Gertrud Buscher.

Hindi

512 **Formal changes in Trinidad Hindi as a result of language adaptation.**
Mridula Adenwala Durbin. *American Anthropologist*, vol. 75, no. 5 (Oct. 1973), p. 1,290-1,304. bibliog.

Durbin studies changes in the structure of Hindi in Trinidad with the aim of seeking explanations for syntactic variations in 'the socio-cultural changes of the East Indian community' on the island. He demonstrates that these socio-cultural changes 'have influenced the range of functions of the Indic languages in Trinidad which in turn has determined the directions of structural changes in the languages.'

Spanish

513 **A preliminary survey of the Spanish dialect of Trinidad.**
Robert Wallace Thompson. *Orbis* (Louvain, Belgium), vol. 6, no. 2 (1957), p. 353-72.

This is the only available article on the Spanish dialect of Trinidad.

Architecture

514 **Tropical Georgian: the great houses and small of the Caribbean.**
Pamela Gosner. Washington, DC: Three Continents Press, 1980. 275p. bibliog.

Described in the publisher's catalogue as the 'first major study of 18th and early 19th century architecture in the Caribbean.' More than two hundred drawings by the author illustrate the architecture of over sixteen islands. Gosner is a member of the Society of Architectural Historians and a professional librarian and artist.

515 **Historic architecture of the Caribbean.**
David Buisseret. London, Kingston, Port-of-Spain: Heinemann, 1980. 93p. map. bibliog.

Buisseret sketches the pre-20th-century architectural history of the non-Hispanic Caribbean in five chapters, each devoted to a category of buildings: domestic, commercial, industrial, military and naval, and religious and public. While Trinidad is mentioned in the volume, the presentation is heavily weighted towards Jamaican architecture. One of the plates illustrating the volume shows the Chase Village Great House in Trinidad.

516 **The elusive deodand: a study of the fortified refuges of the Lesser Antilles.**
David Buisseret. *Journal of Caribbean History*, vol. 6 (May 1973), p. 43-80. maps.

A 'deodand' is a fortification meant to serve as a refuge for non-combatants (or as a final citadel for combatants). Buisseret considers a number of these fort-types in the Caribbean, among them Tobago's Fort King George and Morne Cotton. The article includes a sketch of the plan of Fort King George.

517 **The architecture of Trinidad and Tobago, 1562-1962.**
Peter Bynoe. Port-of-Spain: Guardian Commercial Printery, 1962. 15p.

In spite of its comprehensive title, this is a fifteen-page illustrated pamphlet.

518 **Trinidad town house; or the rise and decline of a domestic architecture.**
Colin Laird. *Caribbean Quarterly*, vol. 3, no. 4 (Aug. 1954), p. 188-98.

Laird discusses the streams of architectural influence that merged in the 1880s to produce a unique building type in Trinidad. A detailed description of one particular house – no. 9, St. Clair Avenue, Port-of-Spain – is provided. The article is illustrated with drawings of various Trinidad houses and building details.

Literature

General history and criticism

519 **West Indian literature: an index to criticism, 1930-1975.**
Jeannette B. Allis. Boston, Massachusetts: G. K. Hall, 1981. 353p. (A Reference Publication in Latin American Studies).

A meticulous bibliographical work, covering writers 'in the geographical region which includes those islands in the Caribbean Sea which were former British possessions (now independent nations) and Guyana.' There are three main sections: an index of authors, an index of critics and reviewers, and an index of general articles from 1933 onwards. The volume locates critical material in journals, newspapers, and essay collections, as well as listing single-author monographs and reviews.

520 **West Indian poetry.**
Lloyd W. Brown. Boston, Massachusetts: Twayne, 1978. 192p. bibliog. (Twayne's World Authors Series, TWAS 422, West Indies).

Brown recounts the history of the poetry of the Caribbean region from 1760 to 1960, and then considers individual poets. Trinidadian poetry is represented in the volume by discussions of the work of the calypsonian 'Sparrow' (Slinger Francisco), on p. 102-06, and of the poetry of Wayne Brown, p. 161-65.

521 **The islands in between: essays on West Indian literature.**
Edited with an introduction by Louis James. London; Ibadan, Nigeria; Nairobi: Oxford University Press, 1968. 166p. bibliog.

James's forty-nine page introduction links literature to the political and cultural situation in which the West Indian writer finds himself, a situation in which, according to James, the West Indian must 'search for his own voice.' James mentions several Trinidadians and their works: Samuel Selvon, C. L. R. James, Alfred Mendes, and Michael Anthony. Among the essays in the body of the book is Gordon Rohlehr's 'The ironic approach; the novels of V. S. Naipaul,' (p. 121-39).

522 **Caribbean literature: the black rock of Africa.**
George Lamming. *African Forum*, vol. 1, no. 4 (Spring 1966), p. 32-52.

The author of the novel *In the castle of my skin* writes about the concept of Africa in the West Indian imagination. Lamming gives examples from West Indian writings of the three elements involved in this idea: 'embarrassment, ambivalence, and a sense of possibility.' Writers from Trinidad and Tobago are mentioned.

523 **The West Indian novelist: prelude and context.**
W. I. Carr. *Caribbean Quarterly*, vol. 11, nos. 1-2 (March-June 1965), p. 71-84.

A perceptive critical discussion of a number of West Indian novelists, viewed against the background of the cultural context in which they write. Carr examines how this context hampers West Indian writers' efforts to construct a truly distinct literature: 'Novelists of the West Indies lack the confidence of a culture either metropolitan or tribal.' Trinidadians V. S. Naipaul and Samuel Selvon are among those mentioned in the article.

524 **The West Indian novel of immigration.**
G. R. Coulthard. *Phylon Quarterly*, vol. 20, no. 1 (First Quarter, Spring 1959), p. 32-41.

One of the novels discussed in this critical article is Samuel Selvon's *Lonely Londoners* (1958), which is set in 'the little world of the West Indian colony in London' whose inhabitants feel aimless and out of place in a white world.

Anthologies

525 **From Trinidad: an anthology of early West Indian writing.**
Edited by Reinhard W. Sander, with the assistance of Peter K. Ayers. New York: Africana Publishing, 1978. 310p.

A collection of writings selected from two Trinidad magazines, *Trinidad*, which was published from 1929 to 1930 and *The Beacon*, which was published from 1931 to 1933. The material anthologized includes editorials, short fiction, poetry, and essays. 'Notes on authors' provides biographical data on the contributors.

526 **Island voices; stories from the West Indies.**
Selected and introduced by Andrew Salkey. New York: Liveright, 1970. 256p.

Salkey, a Jamaican writer, provides a brief but insightful introduction to these contemporary short stories. Stories by Trinidadians included in the volume are V. S. Naipaul's 'My aunt's gold teeth,' 'The raffle,' and 'A Christmas story'; Samuel Selvon's 'Man, in England you've just got to love animals,' 'When Greek meets Greek,' 'Gussy and the boss,' and 'Cane is Bitter'; Michael Anthony's 'The valley of cocoa,' and 'Pita of the deep sea'; C. L. R. James's 'Triumph,' and 'La Divina Pastora'; and Cecil Gray's 'Set this down.' The volume was originally published by Elek Books, London, in 1965, under the title *Stories from the Caribbean*.

527 **Caribbean verse; an anthology.**
Edited and introduced by O. R. Dathorne. London: Heinemann Educational Books, 1967. Reprinted, 1980. 131p.

Dathorne's fifteen page introduction charts the course of West Indian poetry from its beginnings to the present. The poems are annotated with critical notes (p. 82-121); biographical notes (p. 122-28) identify the poets; and there is an index of titles and first lines. Trinidad and Tobago is represented by C. L. Herbert's 'And the pouis sing'; Ian McDonald's 'Jaffo the calypsonian'; Eric Roach's 'Ballad of canga,' and 'To my mother'; and Harold M. Telemaque's 'Poem,' and 'Roots.'

528 **Caribbean narrative; an anthology of West Indian writing.**
Edited and introduced by O. A. Dathorne. London: Heinemann, 1966. Reprinted, 1979. 247p.

Comprises representative selections from Anglophone West Indian imaginative prose writing, intended as an introduction to this work for 'younger readers at pre-university and university stage.' Dathorne's preface gives a brief sketch of West Indian prose from the *Letters* of Sancho (1782) to the 1960s. Trinidadians included are V. S. Naipaul and Samuel Selvon.

Selected works of individual writers

Michael Anthony

529 **Green days by the river.**
Michael Anthony, introduction by Gareth Griffiths. London: Heinemann, 1973. 192p. (Caribbean Writers Series, no. 9).

First published in 1967, this novel, like Anthony's *Year in San Fernando* (q.v.), concerns a boy growing up in Trinidad.

530 **The year in San Fernando.**
Michael Anthony, introduction by Paul Edwards, Kenneth Ramchand. London: Heinemann, 1970. 184p. (Caribbean Writers Series).

Anthony's 1965 novel centres around a twelve-year-old Trinidadian village boy, Francis, and the year he spends in urban San Fernando.

531 **The games were coming.**
Michael Anthony, introduction by Kenneth Ramchand, study questions by Jean D'Costa. London: Heinemann, 1977. 107p. (Caribbean Writers Series, no. 17).

Anthony's first novel, originally published in 1963.

C. L. R. James

532 **Minty Alley.**
C. L. R. James, introduction by Kenneth Ramchand. London: New Beacon Books, 1971. 244p.

First published in 1936, this is the only novel by the Trinidadian Marxist intellectual.

Seepersad Naipaul

533 **The adventures of Gurudeva and other stories.**
Seepersad Naipaul, with a foreword by V. S. Naipaul. London: Deutsch, 1976. 200p.

Short stories of Trinidad's East Indian community by the father of V. S. Naipaul, who provides an introduction to this reissue of the book first published in Trinidad.

Shiva Naipaul

534 **The chip-chip gatherers.**
Shiva Naipaul. New York: Knopf, 1973. 319p.

In this novel Shiva Naipaul, V. S. Naipaul's younger brother, tells the story of two Trinidadian East Indian families, the Ramsarans and the Bholais.

535 **Fireflies.**
Shiva Naipaul. New York: Knopf, 1971. 436p.
Shiva Naipaul's first novel traces the fortunes of three generations of the Khojas, a Hindu family in Trinidad.

V. S. Naipaul

536 **Finding the center: two narratives.**
V. S. Naipaul. New York: Knopf, 1984. 176p.
The volume consists of two long essays, both of which first appeared in the *New Yorker*. In 'Prologue to an autobiography,' Naipaul considers his own life and in 'The crocodiles of Yamoussoukro' he relates his travels in the Ivory Coast.

537 **Three novels.**
V. S. Naipaul. New York: Knopf, 1982. 502p.
A reissue of Naipaul's three earliest volumes of fiction: *The mystic masseur*, *The suffrage of Elvira*, and *Miguel Street*. All three are set in Trinidad.

538 **A bend in the river.**
V. S. Naipaul. New York: Knopf, 1979. 278p.
In this acclaimed novel set in modern Africa, Naipaul paints a powerful picture of post-colonial desperation.

539 **Guerrillas.**
V. S. Naipaul. New York: Knopf, 1975. 248p.
A tense Caribbean island is the scene for the working out of the racial, political, and sexual obsessions of two men and a woman, in a novel that has been called Naipaul's *Heart of darkness*.

540 **In a free state.**
V. S. Naipaul. New York: Knopf, 1971. 256p.
Travel essays, two short stories, and a novella, all focusing on experiences of people trapped in alien cultures, comprise this volume, which was the winner of the 1971 Booker Prize.

541 **The mimic men.**
V. S. Naipaul. Harmondsworth, England: Penguin, 1969. 250p.
This chronicle of the rise and fall of a West Indian politician, first published in 1967, was the winner of the 1968 W. H. Smith Award.

542 **A flag on the island.**
V. S. Naipaul. New York: Macmillan, 1967. 235p.
Eleven short stories, set in Trinidad and London.

543 **Mr. Stone and the Knights Companion.**
V. S. Naipaul. Harmondsworth, England; New York: Penguin, 1973, ca. 1963. 125p.

Perhaps the least known of Naipaul's novels, this is the first of Naipaul's works to be set in England. The book's hero, Mr. Stone, is a soon-to-be-retired librarian who marries at sixty-two, with unforeseen results.

544 **A house for Mr. Biswas.**
V. S. Naipaul. London: Deutsch, 1961. 531p.

The life of Mohun Biswas is recounted in this Dickensian comedy set among the East Indians of Trinidad.

545 **Miguel Street.**
V. S. Naipaul. London: Deutsch, 1959. Reprinted, London: Heinemann, 1974. 222p. (Caribbean Writers Series, no. 14).

The winner of the Somerset Maugham Award, this is a bittersweet collection of comico-satirical short stories set in Port-of-Spain.

546 **The suffrage of Elvira.**
V. S. Naipaul. London: Deutsch, 1958. 240p.

A satire on political change, as symbolized by an election in a Trinidad village.

547 **The mystic masseur.**
V. S. Naipaul, introduction by Paul Edwards, Kenneth Ramchand. London: Heinemann, 1971, 215p. (Caribbean Writers Series, no. 3).

Naipaul's first published novel, which originally appeared in 1957, is a light, satirical comedy with a Trinidadian background. The hero of the book is Ganesh Ramsumair; Naipaul charts Ganesh's zig-zag career as it veers from teaching to massage to mysticism to politics.

Samuel Selvon

548 **Moses migrating.**
Samuel Selvon. Harlow, Essex: Longman, 1983. 186p. (Drumbeat Novels).

The West Indian protagonist of Selvon's *Lonely Londoners* and *Moses ascending* returns to the Caribbean.

549 **Turn again tiger.**
Samuel Selvon, introduction and study questions by Sandra Pouchet Paquet. London: Heinemann, 1979. 182p. (Caribbean Writers Series, no. 19).
A novel set among the East Indians in Trinidad.

550 **Moses ascending.**
Samuel Selvon. London: Davis-Poynter, 1975. 149p.
The West Indian emigrant hero of *The lonely Londoners* now owns a house in Shepherd's Bush.

551 **Those who eat the cascadura.**
Samuel Selvon. London: Davis-Poynter, 1972. 182p.
A rural Caribbean village provides the background for this novel.

552 **A brighter sun; a novel.**
Samuel Selvon. Trinidad: Longmans Caribbean, 1971. 215p.
First published in 1952.

553 **The plains of Caroni.**
Samuel Selvon. London: MacGibbon & Kee, 1970. 166p.
A novel about Trinidad's East Indians in the island's sugar industry.

554 **Ways of sunlight.**
Samuel Selvon. London: MacGibbon & Kee, 1957. 188p.
A collection of short stories.

555 **The lonely Londoners.**
Samuel Selvon. London: A. Wingate, 1956. 171p.
Portrays West Indian immigrants in London.

556 **An island is a world.**
Samuel Selvon. London: A. Wingate, 1955. 288p.
West Indian setting.

Criticism of individual writers

Michael Anthony

557 **The art of memory: Michael Anthony's *The year in San Fernando*.**
Paul Edwards, Kenneth Ramchand. *Journal of Commonwealth Literature*, no. 7 (July 1969), p. 59-72.

A close textual reading of Anthony's novel.

C. L. R. James

558 **Discovering literature in Trinidad: two experiences.**
C. L. R. James, Michael Anthony. *Journal of Commonwealth Literature*, no. 7 (July 1969), p. 73-87.

An edited version of two talks given at a conference in September, 1967. James discusses his formative intellectual experiences in Trinidad in the 1930s; Anthony titles his contribution 'Growing up in writing,' and recollects his boyhood writing in the 1940s.

V. S. Naipaul

559 **V. S. Naipaul and politics: his view of Third World societies in Africa and the Caribbean.**
Helen Pyne-Timothy. *CLA Journal*, vol. 28, no. 3 (March 1985), p. 247-62.

'. . . Naipaul is now regarded internationally as the foremost expositor of Third World political philosophy, attitudes, and movements. This paper attempts to set out what, according to Naipaul, these attitudes might be, what their motivations are, and how they might be evaluated. Finally, an attempt is made to assess the kinds of contribution which Naipaul makes to a larger understanding of the Third World political person.' Pyne-Thomas examines *The mimic men* (1967), *Guerrillas* (1980), *In a free state* (1978), and *A bend in the river* (1979). She finds Naipaul negative and pessimistic about Third World politics.

560 **V. S. Naipaul: a study in expatriate sensibility.**
Sudha Rai. New Delhi: Arnold-Heinemann, 1982. 136p.

An Indian viewpoint on Naipaul as expatriate.

561 **Naipaul: the mimic man.**
Angus Richmond. *Race & Class*, vol. 24, no. 2 (Autumn 1982), p. 125-36.

This article deals with the politics of race in Naipaul's work, particularly as expressed in *The mimic men*, *The Middle Passage*, and *Guerrillas*.

562 **The artist in colonial society: *The mimic men* and *The interpreters*.**
Bruce MacDonald. *Caribbean Quarterly*, vol. 28, nos. 1-2 (March-June 1982), p. 20-31.

In this critique linking V. S. Naipaul's *The mimic men* and Wole Soyinka's *The interpreters*, MacDonald concentrates on the aesthetic problems faced by the novelist who attempt to portray the 'geographical schizophrenia of the colonial experience.'

563 **Critical perspectives on V. S. Naipaul.**
Edited by Robert D. Hamner. Washington, DC: Three Continents Press, 1977. 300p. bibliog. (Critical Perspectives, no. 2).

A collection of critical essays on Naipaul as novelist and essayist, which also includes a thirty-four page bibliography.

564 **Revolutionary struggle and the novel.**
Selwyn R. Cudjoe. *Caribbean Quarterly*, vol. 25, no. 4 (Dec. 1979), p. 1-30.

Cudjoe contends that 'revolutionary struggle in the novel is utilized with a well-defined intention.' He illustrates this idea by analysing three novels with revolutionary themes: Bertene Juminer's *Bozambo's revenge*, V. S. Naipaul's *Guerrillas*, and Alejo Carpentier's *Explosion in a cathedral*. Cudjoe's view of Naipaul is largely unfavourable.

565 **'A vision of the land': V. S. Naipaul's later novels.**
John Cooke. *Caribbean Quarterly*, vol. 25, no. 4 (Dec. 1979), p. 31-47.

Cooke states that 'the search for histories in the landscape becomes the focus of Naipaul's later novels. It is the tension between this search and Naipaul's abiding belief that nothing had been created in the West Indies or in Africa . . . that shapes *The mimic men* (1967), *In a free state* (1971), and *Guerrillas* (1975). This tension is resolved by *A bend in the river* (1979) . . . [which] clearly marks the end of Naipaul's twenty-year examination of his "new world" landscapes for a native historical tradition.'

566 **The snow virgin: an inquiry into V. S. Naipaul's *Mimic men*.**
John Hearne. *Caribbean Quarterly*, vol. 23, nos. 2-3 (June-Sept. 1977), p. 31-37.

This article presents one Caribbean writer's evaluation of another. The Jamaican novelist Hearne calls Naipaul's *Mimic men* 'an authentic work of art without a shred of hope,' writing that it is 'a good book with a despair so isolate, with a privacy so armoured against any intrusion of society, that we can do no more than concede the unremitting integrity of its pessimism.'

567 **V. S. Naipaul.**
Michael Thorpe, edited by Ian Scott-Kilvert. London: Published for the British Council by Longman Group, 1976. 47p. bibliog.

A pamphlet summarizing the life and work of Naipaul up to the publication of *Guerrillas* (1975). Besides listing Naipaul's books, articles, and reviews, the bibliography also includes interviews given by Naipaul and selected critical studies of his work.

568 **Paradoxes of order; some perspectives on the fiction of V. S. Naipaul.**
Robert K. Morris. Columbia, Missouri: University of Missouri Press, 1975. 105p.

A lengthy interpretative essay on Naipaul's fiction, up to *In a free state* (1971).

569 **V. S. Naipaul and the colonial image.**
Michael V. Angrosino. *Caribbean Quarterly*, vol. 21, no. 3 (Sept. 1975), p. 1-11. bibliog.

In this general review of Naipaul's work, Angrosino comments on the ambivalent feelings that Naipaul as an 'escaped' Trinidadian has towards his native island. Includes a bibliography of Naipaul's books.

570 **V. S. Naipaul's negative sense of place.**
Keith Garebian. *Journal of Commonwealth Literature*, vol. 10, no. 1 (Aug. 1975), p. 23-35.

Discusses 'Naipaulia' – Naipaul's 'settings which project perpetual confusion' and lack a 'sense of psychological harmony.'

571 **V. S. Naipaul's starting point.**
Anthony Boxill. *Journal of Commonwealth Literature*, vol. 10, no. 1 (Aug. 1975), p. 1-9.

Boxill detects a source for V. S. Naipaul's writings in *Gurudeva and other Indian tales*, seven short stories written by his father, Seepersad Naipaul, and published in Port-of-Spain. Boxill analyses the elder Naipaul's stories and points out ways in which they parallel his son's fiction.

572 **V. S. Naipaul's Third World: a not so free state.**
John Thieme. *Journal of Commonwealth Literature*, vol. 10, no. 1 (Aug. 1975), p. 10-22.

Thieme discusses V. S. Naipaul's controversial feelings and statements about the former colonial world. Unlike most commentators on this aspect of Naipaul's work, Thieme feels that Naipaul does evince sympathy for the Third World and that his view of it is not entirely negative.

573 **V. S. Naipaul: a selected bibliography.**
Robert D. Hamner. *Journal of Commonwealth Literature*, vol. 10, no. 1 (Aug. 1975), p. 36-44.

A useful list of Naipaul's writings and of commentaries on his work up to 1972. Unannotated entries are grouped into primary and secondary sources. Primary sources include books, articles, and short stories, excluding book reviews by Naipaul. Secondary sources include book reviews, books, and articles on Naipaul's work.

574 **V. S. Naipaul.**
Robert D. Hamner. New York: Twayne, 1973. 181p. bibliog. (Twayne's World Authors Series. TWAS 258. West Indies).

A basic literary interpretation in the usual format of this series.

575 **V. S. Naipaul; an introduction to his work.**
Paul Theroux. New York: Africana Publishing Corporation, 1972. 144p. bibliog.

The American novelist and travel-writer discusses both Naipaul's fictional and non-fictional works. The book is organized into chapters each of which treats a Naipaulian theme: creation, fantasy, marriage and the householder, rootlessness and travel, and a sense of the past. In a final chapter, Theroux comments on Naipaul's style.

576 **Commentary on V. S. Naipaul's *A house for Mr. Biswas*; 1. A West Indian epic.**
Barry Argyle. *Caribbean Quarterly*, vol. 16, no. 4 (Dec. 1970), p. 61-69.

An essay that enumerates the novel's epic features.

577 **[Commentary on V. S. Naipaul's *A house for Mr. Biswas*]; 2. Cultural confrontation, disintegration, and syncretism in *A house for Mr. Biswas*.**
Maureen Warner. *Caribbean Quarterly*, vol. 16, no. 4 (Dec. 1970), p. 70-79.

Warner concentrates on the theme of cultural clash which she sees as central to Naipaul's novel.

578 **Naipaul's technique as a novelist.**
A. C. Derrick. *Journal of Commonwealth Literature*, no. 7 (July 1969), p. 32-44.

A discussion of the overall design and mode of presentation in Naipaul's pre-1963 novels.

579 **The world of *A house for Mr. Biswas.***
Kenneth Ramchand. *Caribbean Quarterly*, vol. 15, no. 1 (March 1969), p. 60-72. bibliog.

A lengthy review article on one of Naipaul's major novels, which is set in Trinidad. Ramchand teaches at the Department of English, University of the West Indies.

580 **V. S. Naipaul and the new order.**
Karl Miller. *Kenyon Review*, vol. 29, no. 5 (Nov. 1967), p. 685-98.

A review of *The mimic men* that sets the novel in the context of Naipaul's other work.

581 **Predestination, frustration and symbolic darkness in Naipaul's *A house for Mr. Biswas.***
F. G. Rohlehr. *Caribbean Quarterly*, vol. 10, no. 1 (March 1964), p. 3-11.

A prize-winning essay. Rohlehr sees as the moral of the novel that 'life after all is not entirely useless, although its ultimate reward may closely resemble failure and frustration.'

Samuel Selvon

582 **Critical perspectives on Sam Selvon.**
Edited by Susheila Nasta. Washington, DC: Three Continents Press, 1985. 280p. (Critical Perspectives Series).

Collected critical essays discussing Selvon's novels and short stories.

583 **Samuel Selvon's linguistic extravaganza: *Moses ascending.***
Maureen Warner-Lewis. *Caribbean Quarterly*, vol. 28, no. 4 (Dec. 1982), p. 60-69.

A critique which emphasizes Selvon's linguistic exuberance and virtuoso handling of language codes and registers in his 1975 humorous novel.

584 **The clown in the slave ship.**
Peter Nazareth. *Caribbean Quarterly*, vol. 23, nos. 2-3 (June-Sept 1977), p. 24-30. bibliog.

A review of Selvon's comic novel *Moses ascending* (1975).

Foreign miscellany

585 **A morning at the office, a novel.**
Edgar Mittelholzer. London: Heinemann, 1974. 256p. (Caribbean Writers Series, no. 11).

This book, published in the USA under the title *A morning in Trinidad*, earned its Guyanese author mixed reviews when it first appeared in 1950. Mittelholzer uses an office in Trinidad during a single morning as a microcosm in which to observe the interplay between race, sex, and class relations in the West Indies.

586 **Murder in Trinidad, a case in the career of Bertram Lynch, P.C.B.**
John W. Vandercook. Garden City, New York: Published for the Crime Club by Doubleday, Doran & Company, 1933. 306p.

This murder mystery with a Trinidadian setting has been reprinted several times, most recently by Collier in 1962. When it first appeared in 1933, a reviewer in the *Saturday Review of Literature* commented on the novel's 'hair-raising action [and] exotic locale.' The book was made into a film in 1934, directed by Louis King and starring Nigel Bruce as the cool but ill-groomed British sleuth, Bertram Lynch.

Theatre, Oratory and Performance Arts

587 **The theatrical into theatre: a study of the drama and theatre of the English-speaking Caribbean.**
Kole Omotoso. London, Port-of-Spain: New Beacon Books, 1982. 173p. bibliog.

Omotoso traces the main developments in the drama of the Caribbean's anglophone Blacks from the pre-abolition theatre and theatrics of carnivals and slave festivals down to the work of modern playwrights, actors and theatrical companies. Includes examination of the work of Trinidad's Errol Hill, Errol Jones and Douglas Archibald.

588 **Forged from the love of liberty: selected speeches of Dr. Eric Williams.**
Eric Williams, edited by Paul Sutton. Port-of-Spain: Longman Caribbean, 1981. Reprinted, London: Longman, 1982. 474p.

Presents the speeches of Trinidad's scholar-politician-statesman and first Prime Minister.

589 **Theme and form in the speeches of Norman Manley and Eric Williams.**
Marian McLeod. *Caribbean Quarterly*, vol. 22, no. 4 (Dec. 1976), p. 79-89. bibliog.

McLeod examines the orations of these two West Indian statesman 'to determine not only the content and form of the ideas, but also the extent to which those ideas are the product of both speakers' own qualities and the influence of the thought and feeling of their time, including the modifying effects exerted by their particular audiences.'

590 **The emergence of a national drama in the West Indies.**
Errol Hill. *Caribbean Quarterly*, vol. 18, no. 4 (Dec. 1972), p. 9-40.

Includes the history of the theatre in Trinidad, placed within the context of the drama of the British West Indies as a whole, from 1832 to the 20th century. Hill discusses C. L. R. James's *Toussaint L'Ouverture*, produced in London in 1936, and the work of Arthur Roberts and DeWilton Rogers. The White Hall Players and other recent drama groups in Trinidad are also mentioned.

591 **Patterns of performance in the British West Indies.**
Roger Abrahams. In: *Afro-American anthropology: contemporary perspectives.* Edited by Norman E. Whitten, Jr., John F. Szwed. London: Collier-Macmillan; New York: Free Press, 1970, p. 163-79.

A study of cultural expression through performance in Black communities. Abrahams states that 'two West Indian island communities, Tobago and Nevis, will be described to illustrate the varieties of [the] man-of-words tradition, how traditional expression harmonizes with the ethos in these communities, and what recent forces have effected changes in folklore, specifically in modifying the performance pattern.' Tobago is dealt with on p. 166-71, focusing on the Speech Mas', a performance troupe unique to that island. A shorter version of this essay appeared in *Trans-Action*, vol. 5, no. 8 (July-Aug. 1968), p. 62-71, under the title 'Public drama and common values in two Caribbean islands.'

Sport

592 **Caribbean cricketers from the pioneers to Packer.**
Clayton Goodwin, with a foreword by Colin Cowdrey. London: Harrap, 1980. 260p. map.

A recent compendium of information on West Indian cricket, which includes a statistical appendix covering test match results, from 1928 to 1979.

593 **Beyond a boundary.**
C. L. R. James, with an introduction by Robert Lipsyte. London: Stanley Paul, 1963. Reprinted, New York: Pantheon Books, 1983. 255p.

A 'one-of-a-kind book,' about cricket, other sports, and social conditions, intertwined with anecdotes on James's life in Trinidad and in England. James states in his preface that 'This book is neither cricket reminiscences nor autobiography. It poses the question What do they know of cricket who only cricket know? The answer involves ideas well as facts.'

594 **Island cricketers.**
Clyde A. Walcott. London: Hodder & Stoughton, 1958. 188p.

Illustrated with fourteen plates.

Libraries and Archives

Within Trinidad and Tobago

595 **Trinidad and Tobago.**
In: *World guide to libraries; Internationales Bibliotheks-Handbuch.* New York, London, Paris: K. G. Saur, 1986. 7th ed. p. 626. (Handbook of International Documentation and Information, vol. 8).

This directory lists national, university and college, special, and public libraries with brief information on the name and address of each library, the year it was founded, the current directory, and the size of its collection.

596 **Research guide to Central America and the Caribbean.**
Editor-in-chief, Kenneth Grieb, associate editors, Ralph Lee Woodward Jr., Graeme S. Mount, Thomas Mathews. Madison, Wisconsin: University of Wisconsin Press, 1985. 431p.

An up-to-date and useful reference tool which identifies archival resources in the Caribbean available to researchers. The 'Trinidad and Tobago' chapter by Bridget Brereton (p. 357-60), describes the libraries and archival collections in Trinidad and Tobago that contain materials of interest. Other references to Trinidadian materials can be located through the index to the volume. Basic information is provided about each institution listed: the scope of the holdings, its unique aspects or restrictions, availability, hours of operation, and prevailing conditions.

597 **A handbook of Latin American and Caribbean National Archives. Guia de los archivos nacionales de America Latina y el Caribe.**
Ann K. Nauman. Detroit, Michigan: Blaine Ethridge Books, 1983. 127p. bibliog.

A first-time user's directory that provides information on materials, services, requirements, and restrictions for each Latin American and Caribbean country's national archives. Data on Trinidad's National Archives in Port-of-Spain, is given in English on p. 47-49 and in Spanish on p. 109-11.

598 **Trinidad and Tobago, libraries.**
Alma Jordan. In: *Encyclopedia of library and information science.* Edited by Allen Kent (et al.). New York; Basel, Switzerland: Marcel Dekker, 1981, vol. 31, p. 137-51. bibliog.

Topics covered are background information, colonial libraries, post-colonial library development, plans for a national library, public libraries, school libraries, university libraries, the Library Association of Trinidad and Tobago, the national bibliography, library education, and the regional library association (Association of Caribbean University and Research Libraries).

599 **The archives of Trinidad and Tobago, British West Indies.**
Gertrude Carmichael. *Archives*, vol. 1, no. 8 (Michaelmas, 1952), p. 39-41.

These few pages in the journal of the British Records Association note that records for Trinidad are sparse before 1816, although the archives contain a few from 1810. Also in the archives is a manuscript index to the missing Spanish records of 1787-1813. Tobagonian records are fairly numerous from 1793 onwards.

600 **Guide to libraries and archives in Central America and the West Indies, Panama, Bermuda, and British Guiana, supplemented with information on private libraries, bookbinding, book selling and printing.**
Arthur E. Groop. New Orleans, Louisiana: Middle American Research Institute, Tulane University of Louisiana, 1941. 721p. map. bibliog. (Tulane University of Louisiana. Middle American Research Institute. Middle American Research Series, Publication, 10).

Although out-dated in the information it provides on practical details of hours and services, this reference work can still be profitably consulted by researchers seeking archival materials. The section on Trinidad and Tobago (p. 321-46), surveys the collections of public and private libraries in the country, as well as the archives of Tobago, of Trinidad in Port-of-Spain, of San Fernando, of the Supreme Court in Port-of-Spain, and of Trinity Cathedral, also in Port-of-Spain.

601 **The libraries of Bermuda, the Bahamas, the British West Indies, British Guiana, British Honduras, Puerto Rico, and the American Virgin Islands; a report to the Carnegie Corporation of New York.**
Ernest A. Savage. London: Library Association, 1934. 102p. bibliog.

This early survey of the libraries of the Anglophone Caribbean may still prove useful to researchers.

Outside Trinidad and Tobago

602 **The catalogue of the West India Reference Library.**
Institute of Jamaica, Kingston, West India Reference Library. Millwood, New York: Kraus International Publications, 1980. 2 vols. in 6.

This catalogue of the collection of what is now the National Library of Jamaica constitutes a retrospective bibliography of the entire West Indies, with many items pertaining to Trinidad and Tobago.

603 **Directory of libraries and special collections on Latin America and the West Indies.**
Bernard Naylor, Laurence Hallewell, Colin Steele. London: Athlone Press for the Institute of Latin American Studies, 1975. 161p. (London. Institute of Latin American Studies. Monograph no. 5).

An up-to-date source for the location of West Indian materials in Great Britain.

604 **Guide to resources for Commonwealth studies in London, Oxford and Cambridge, with bibliographical and other information.**
A. R. Hewitt. London: University of London, Athlone Press for the Institute of Commonwealth Studies, 1957. 219p. bibliog.

This excellent work remains justifiably in print nearly thirty years after it was first published. It lists institutional and library resources for the study of the Commonwealth, mainly in the areas of history and the social sciences, to be found in London, Oxford and Cambridge. Includes sections on the West Indies and on Trinidad.

605 **Subject catalogue of the Library of the Royal Empire Society.**
Evans Lewin. Royal Empire Society, 1932. Reprinted, with a new introduction by Donald H. Simpson. London: Dawsons for the Royal Commonwealth Society, 1967. 4 vols.

A comprehensive bibliography of the British Empire up to 1930. It includes carefully catalogued listings of periodical articles and government papers as well as books. Volume three includes the British West Indies in general (p. 503-45), with a specific Trinidad and Tobago section (p. 588-98).

Mass Media

General

606 **The 'Caribbean man': a study in the psychology of perception and the media.**

Ramesh Deosaran. *Caribbean Quarterly*, vol. 27, nos. 2-3 (June-Sept. 1981), p. 60-89. bibliog.

A study of the controversy over the calypso 'Caribbean unity,' popularly known as 'Caribbean man,' which, sung by the calypsonian Black Stalin, won the islands' Calypso Monarch Competition in 1979. The song subsequently ignited a nationwide dispute on the question of whether the lyrics describing the 'Caribbean man' were intended to apply only to those of African descent, excluding other Trinidadian ethnic groups, specifically the East Indians. Deosaran sketches in the background of the controversy, follows the progress of the dispute through editorials and letters in Trinidad's newspapers, and analyses the problem of Caribbean identity and its implications for race relations in the country. The article includes a transcript of the provocative calypso.

607 **Caribbean mass communications; a comprehensive bibliography.**

John A. Lent. Waltham, Massachusetts: Crossroads Press, African Studies Association, 1981. 152p. (Archival and Bibliographic Series).

A basic and useful reference tool. The Trinidad and Tobago section (p. 56-65) contains over 250 bibliographical references to books, periodical articles, and newspaper articles on the country's mass communications, broadcasting, film, freedom of the press, history of the press, and print media. Most of the entries are unannotated.

608 **Mass media roles in electoral campaigns: the Trinidad and Tobago 1976 General Election.**

S. Nancoo. *Indian Journal of Political Studies*, vol. 2, no. 2 (July 1978), p. 118-29.

Underlines the important role played by the mass media in Trinidadian politics.

609 **Commonwealth Caribbean: production and consumption of mass media.**

John A. Lent. *Caribbean Studies*, vol. 16, no. 2 (July 1976), p. 184-218.

A broad survey which, the author states, 'will concentrate on the media production and consumption factors in the islands, as well as two closely related subjects: capital investment needed to start and sustain media production, and social overhead services necessary in the production, transmission and reception of media messages.' Sections cover investment and maintenance capital; plant and equipment; personnel; literacy and motivation; affordability. The article refers to the printed media, radio and television in Trinidad as well as the rest of the Anglophone Caribbean. Based largely on personal interviews with area editors and newspaper managers.

610 **Commonwealth Caribbean mass media: history and development.**

John A. Lent. *Gazette: International Journal for Mass Communications Studies*, vol. 19, no. 2 (1973), p. 91-106.

A survey of regional mass media, based on research in the area in 1968, 1970, and 1971. Includes references to Trinidad, mentioning the first newspaper on the island (the weekly *Gaceta*), and commenting on the growth of newspaper publishing there. After an historical overview, Lent discusses present-day Caribbean media, including Trinidad's *Guardian*, *Evening News*, *Express*, and *Sunday Guardian*, and radio and television on the island.

Newspapers and journalism

611 **Business interests, freedom of the press and Grenada.**

Carl D. Parris. *Caribbean Quarterly*, vol. 27, nos. 2-3 (June-Sept. 1981), p. 28-39.

Examines the confrontation between the Government of Grenada and two newspaper publishing companies operating in Trinidad and Tobago: the Trinidad Express Newspapers, Ltd., publisher of the *Express*, the *Sunday Express*, and the *Sun*; and the Trinidad Publishing Company, Ltd., which publishes the Trinidad *Guardian*, the *Sunday Guardian*, and the *Evening News*. The conflict took place over the government's shutting-down of the *Torchlight* newspaper on Grenada, an organ in which the Trinidad Express Newspapers, Ltd., held minority shares.

612 **The oldest existing newspapers in the Commonwealth Caribbean.**
John A. Lent. *Caribbean Quarterly*, vol. 22, no. 4 (Dec. 1976), p. 90-106. bibliog.

A valuable enumeration of all known newspapers, current or defunct, in the Commonwealth Caribbean. The Trinidad and Tobago segment (p. 100-02), lists the islands' newspapers from the pre-1790 *Gaceta* down to the 1969 *Tapia*. For each paper named, the date it was founded, its frequency of publication, and the year of its last known issue are provided.

Printing and publishing

613 **Educational publishing and book production in the English-speaking Caribbean.**
Alvona Alleyne, Pam Mordecai. *Library Trends*, vol. 26, no. 4 (Spring 1978), p. 575-89. bibliog.

The authors survey the region's educational publishing at all levels – primary, secondary, and tertiary – concentrating mainly on Guyana, Jamaica, and Trinidad. The article also furnishes informative facts on the Caribbean's periodical press.

614 **The first printing on the island of Tobago.**
Douglas C. McMurtrie. Fort Worth, Texas: National Association for Printing Education, 1943. 4p.

This pamphlet is a reprint of an item that appeared in the *National Printing Education Journal* (April, 1943). A more recent article on the subject is Edwina Peters Roberts's 'Printing in Tobago,' which appeared in *Working Papers on West Indian Printing*, series 2 (Mona, Jamaica: Dept. of Library Studies, University of the West Indies, 1976).

615 **Notes on the beginning of printing on the island of Trinidad.**
Douglas C. McMurtie. Forth Worth, Texas: National Association for Printing Education, 1943. 6p.

Printing began on Trinidad with the publication of a *Gaceta* in 1789, while the island was still under the political jurisdiction of the Captain generalcy of Venezuela. This essay by McMurtrie was originally published in the *National Printing Education Journal* (May, 1943). More recently several essays on the history of printing in Trinidad have been published in the *Working Papers on West Indian Printing* of the Dept. of Library Studies, University of the West Indies. In series one (1974-1975), appeared two articles by Roderick Cave: 'Note on the introduction of printing to Trinidad de Barlovento by Edward W. Daniel (1950) with additional notes by R. Cave,' and 'The history of printing in Trinidad: some preliminary notes.' In series two (1976), appeared Cave's 'Early printing in southern Trinidad.'

Newspapers

616 **Sun.**

Port-of-Spain, 1978- . daily.

Publisher Ken Gordon claims a circulation of 23,000 for the *Sun*, Trinidad and Tobago's most-recently established still-active evening daily.

617 **Express.**

Port-of-Spain, 1967- . daily.

This morning paper with a circulation of 69,000 is also published by Ken Gordon. Competes with the *Guardian* both as a morning paper and with its Sunday edition.

618 **Evening News.**

Port-of-Spain, 1936- . daily.

Published by Mark A Conyers, the evening 'sister' paper of the morning *Guardian* has a circulation of approximately 33,000.

619 **Guardian.**

Port-of-Spain, 1917- . daily.

The *grande dame* of Trinidad's newspapers. Although the circulation of its weekday edition (approximately 51,000) is now second to that of the *Express*, its Sunday edition has a circulation of nearly 88,000 – close to one-tenth of the total population of Trinidad and Tobago. As the *Trinidad Guardian*, its editorial policy represented the viewpoint of the conservative white or near-white businessman, making the paper a favourite target of Eric Williams, who attacked it regularly in his *PNM Weekly*.

Reference Works

620 **Trinidad and Tobago.**
In: *The World of Learning, 1984-85.* London: Europa Publications, 1985. p. 1,164.

An annually updated brief listing of learned societies, research institutes, libraries, museums, and institutions of higher education. Entries provide names, addresses, directors, chief personnel, publications, and miscellaneous directory information.

621 **Caribbean telephone directory.**
West Falmouth, Massachusetts: Caribbean Imprint Library Services, 1983-84. 704p.

A business directory for the Caribbean region with entries arranged under 600 alphabetical categories, from Abrasive Materials to Zippers. Names, addresses, and telephone numbers are provided.

622 **Personalities Caribbean; the international guide to who's who in the West Indies, Bahamas, Bermuda.**
Edited by Anthony Lancelot Levy, Hedley Powell Jacobs. Kingston: Personalities, 1983. 7th ed. 1,027p.

Provides standard biographical information on notable living persons with some entries accompanied by photographs. The volume is revised every two years. The Trinidad and Tobago section is on p. 567-708.

623 **Caribbean Year Book, 1979/80.**
Toronto: Caribook, annual. 922p.

Until 1977, this annual publication was known as *The West Indies and Caribbean Year Book*. It is a compilation of facts supplied by individuals and government ministries. 'Trinidad and Tobago' (p. 745-89), contains sections on climate, topography, political geography, population, government, public and social services, public utilities, communications, natural resources, industries, finance, economic development, diplomatic and consular affairs, trade and tourist information, and newspapers and periodicals. Business directory information is also provided.

624 **Caribbean writers; a bio-bibliographical-critical encyclopedia.**
Edited by Donald E. Herdeck, Maurice A. Lubin, John Figueroa, Dorothy A. Figueroa, Jose Alcantara, Margaret L. Herdeck. Washington, DC: Three Continents Press, 1979. 943p. bibliog.

A fundamental reference work on Caribbean literature that pulls together much difficult-to-locate material. Each writer receives a capsule biography followed by a bibliography that lists both the subject's own work and critical studies. The various language groups are dealt with separately: the Anglophone literature section includes an 'Essay on West Indian writing' that discusses the literature of the English-speaking Caribbean and a country-by-country listing of writers from the formerly-British East Indies. The volume also contains seven excellent bibliographies on the Anglophone Caribbean: West Indian literature and culture: bibliographies; The West Indies: critical studies; West Indian literature: general anthologies and collections; literature pre-1900; background books (selected); historical writings pre-1900; background books (selected); general background studies on various island post-1900; and West Indian literature: selected journals.

625 **Historical dictionary of the British Caribbean.**
William Lux. Metuchen, New Jersey: Scarecrow Press, 1975. 266p. bibliog. (Latin American Historical Dictionaries, no. 12).

Trinidad and Tobago is covered on p. 191-223. Short, informative entries, are in alphabetical order, from Abbey School to Woodford, Sir Ralph. Includes a complete list of the governors of Trinidad, 1520-1972.

Bibliographies

Current

626 **The CARICOM bibliography.**
Georgetown: Library of the Secretariat of the Caribbean Community, 1977- . annual.

A bibliography of materials published in the Caribbean Community member territories, which includes Trinidad and Tobago. The volume is arranged in two sections, author/title and subject. It lists books and the first issues of periodicals.

627 **Trinidad and Tobago National Bibliography.**
Port-of-Spain: Central Library of Trinidad and Tobago, 1975- . quarterly.

This is the successor to the *Trinidad and Tobago and West Indian Bibliography: Monthly Accessions* (1966-1975), which in turn replaced the *Classified List of Accessions* issued in mimeographed form by the West Indian Reference Collection of the Trinidad and Tobago Central Library from 1965 to 1966. Lists material printed and published in Trinidad and Tobago. The main listing is by Dewey Decimal classification with author, title, and series indexes. Includes a directory of Trinidad and Tobago's publishers. During its early years, cumulations appeared at irregular intervals and covered four to six month periods; since 1968, however, cumulations are published annually and cover an entire year.

628 **Caribbean Studies.**
Rio Piedras, Puerto Rico: Institute of Caribbean Studies, University of Puerto Rico, 1961- . quarterly.

The 'Current bibliography' in each issue of this scholarly journal is a 'selected compilation of current books, periodical literature and certain documentary material of interest to Caribbeanists.'

629 **Handbook of Latin American studies.**
Edited by Dolores Moyano Martin (et al.). Cambridge, Massachusetts: Harvard University Press, 1936-51. Gainesville, Florida: University of Florida Press, 1952-79. Austin, Texas; London: University of Texas Press, 1980- .

HLAS is the basic source for current Latin American bibliography, including the anglophone countries of the Caribbean region. Since 1965, the work has been published in two volumes appearing in alternate years, one volume covering the social sciences and its companion, the humanities. Entries are annotated by scholars with reviews of subject literature often provided by authorities. Books, periodical articles, pamphlets, and conference papers in all major languages are included. Annotations are in English or Spanish. A cumulative author index to the first thirty years of the publication has been compiled by Francisco José and Maria Elena Cardona (*Author index to Handbook of Latin American studies, nos. 1-28, 1936-1966*, Gainesville, Florida: University of Florida, 1968).

Retrospective

630 **The English-speaking Caribbean: a bibliography of bibliographies.**
Alma Jordan, Barbara Comissiong. Boston, Massachusetts: G. K. Hall, 1984. 436p.

This welcome attempt at bibliographic control contains more than 4,000 annotated entries to both published and unpublished bibliographies listing materials on the Anglophone Caribbean. Main arrangement is by broad subject classification; bibliographic material on Trinidad and Tobago can be located through the index.

631 **Latin America and the Caribbean II: a dissertation bibliography.**
Marian C. Walters. Ann Arbor, Michigan: University Microfilms International, 1980. 78p.

This supplements and updates *Latin America and the Caribbean: a dissertation bibliography* (q.v.) and follows the organization of the earlier volume.

632 **Latin America and the Caribbean; a dissertation bibliography.**
Carl W. Deal. Ann Arbor, Michigan: University Microfilms International, 1978. 164p.

Available gratis from the publisher, this work lists more than 7,200 theses completed up to and including 1977 that are available from University Microfilms. The work is arranged by subject with an author index.

633 **The complete Caribbeana, 1975; a bibliographic guide to the scholarly literature.**
Lambros Comitas. Millwood, New York: KTO Press, 1977. 4 vols.

The major retrospective source for non-Hispanic Caribbean bibliography, this publication is an expansion of Comitas's *Caribbeana, 1900-1965* (Seattle, Washington: University of Washington Press for the Research Institute for the Study of Man, 1968). The work is organized in four volumes: volume one, People; volume two, Institutions; volume three, Resources; and volume four, Indexes. The plan of the work is topical: there are nine major thematic sections and sixty-three topical chapters. The work contains 17,000 citations to all types of printed materials on 'those mainland and insular possessions or former possessions of Great Britain, France, the Netherlands, and the United States in the Caribbean region.' Trinidad and Tobago is included. Each bibliographic citation includes the location of the item. There are no annotations. The work is indexed by author, subject, and geographical location.

634 **Caribbean studies, part I.**
Edith F. Hurwitz.. *Choice*, vol. 12, no. 4 (June 1975), p. 487-502. bibliog.

A narrative bibliographical essay with a 'Works cited' list appended which provides bibliographical details. Consists largely of materials in history and the social sciences. There are general studies of the Caribbean region, followed by the Commonwealth Caribbean, with both general studies and studies on specific nations. Trinidad and Tobago receives two paragraphs. The work is highly selective, but relatively up-to-date.

635 **Theses on the Commonwealth Caribbean, 1891-1973.**
Commonwealth Caribbean Resource Centre. London, Ontario: Office of International Education, University of Western Ontario, 1974. 136p.

Dissertations accepted in the universities of Great Britain, the United States, and Canada. There is an author listing and a geographical index.

636 **Theses on Caribbean topics 1778-1968.**
Enid M. Baa. San Juan: Institute of Caribbean Studies and the University of Puerto Rico, 1970. 146p. bibliog. (Caribbean Bibliographic Series, no. 1).

The main body of the work is a list of doctoral dissertations, arranged alphabetically by author, to which is added a similar listing of Masters and other theses. Four indexes allow the user to locate items by the university at which the dissertation was written; the country studied in the dissertation; the general subject of the dissertation; and the year that the dissertation was written. Coverage is most complete for theses submitted to universities in the United States, England, and France. Seventy-two dissertations referring to Trinidad and Tobago are listed.

637 **Latin America and the Caribbean; a bibliographical guide to works in English.**
S. A. Bayitch. Coral Gables, Florida: University of Miami Press; Dobbs Ferry, New York: Oceana Publications, 1967. 943p. (University of Miami School of Law: Interamerican Legal Studies, vol. 10).

An older, retrospective social-science-oriented bibliography. Of interest to Trinidadists are sections on the Caribbean (p. 265-89), the British West Indies (p. 803-65), and Trinidad and Tobago (p. 858-65). Brief, unannotated entries list books, periodical articles, and government reports. There are references to texts of Trinidad's constitutions from 1875 to 1952. The work also lists statutes, ordinances and court reports.

638 **A bibliography of neo-African literature from Africa, America and the Caribbean.**
Janheinz Jahn. London: Andre Deutsch, 1965. 359p.

This bibliography of 'the new literature of African culture' is an unannotated listing of the creative literary work of individual authors, including plays and essays. Anthologies are noted in a separate section. Trinidadians included are Michael Anthony, Douglas Archibald, Ralph de Boissiere, Cecil Gray, Errol G. Hill, Geoffrey Holder, C. L. R. James, Errol G. John, Charles Anthony Lynch, Alfred Mendes, V. S. Naipaul, Samuel Selvon, and Harold M. Telemaque.

639 **A West Indian book collection.**
Eric Williams. *Caribbean Commission Monthly Information Bulletin*, vol. 6, no. 3 (Oct. 1952), p. 59-62; 72.

A superior narrative presentation of basic books for the study of West Indian history and culture, covering British, French, and Spanish materials, by Trinidad's Eric Williams, who was then Deputy Chairman of the Caribbean Research Council.

640 **Caribbean bookshelf.**
[No author]. *Caribbean Quarterly*, vol. 1, no. 4 ([no month given, no year given: 1950?]), p. 45-47.

An unannotated list of standard and general books on the British Caribbean 'published for those who are beginning to study the history of the British Caribbean.'

641 **Bibliography of the West Indies (excluding Jamaica).**
Frank Cundall. Kingston: Institute of Jamaica, 1909. Reprinted, New York, London: Johnson Reprint Corporation, 1971. 179p.

A pioneering effort in West Indian bibliography by a librarian at the Institute of Jamaica, this work is based on the collection at the Institute as of 1909. Items which are not in the Institute's Library are asterisked. The bibliography follows a chronological arrangement under geographical divisions, with four additional sections dealing with general topics: West Indies generally; Slavery; Buccaneers;

British West Africa; and Parliamentary Papers relating to the West Indies generally. The last category lists Pariamentary Papers from 1750 to 1900. Books, pamphlets, and government reports are listed with abbreviated titles, there are no annotations. The bibliography is indexed by name of authors, subjects of memoirs, and cartographers. The Trinidad section (p. 89-91), includes approximately sixty items, published between 1802 and 1900. Tobago receives a single page (p. 92), listing twelve titles, from 1665 to 1906.

Index

The index is a single alphabetical sequence of authors (personal and corporate), titles of publications and subjects. Index entries refer both to the main items and to other works mentioned in the notes to each item. Title entries are in italics. Numeration refers to the items as numbered.

B

C

F

G

H

J

K

M

N

Q

R

S

T

U

V

W

Y

Z

Map of Trinidad and Tobago

This map shows the more important towns and other features.

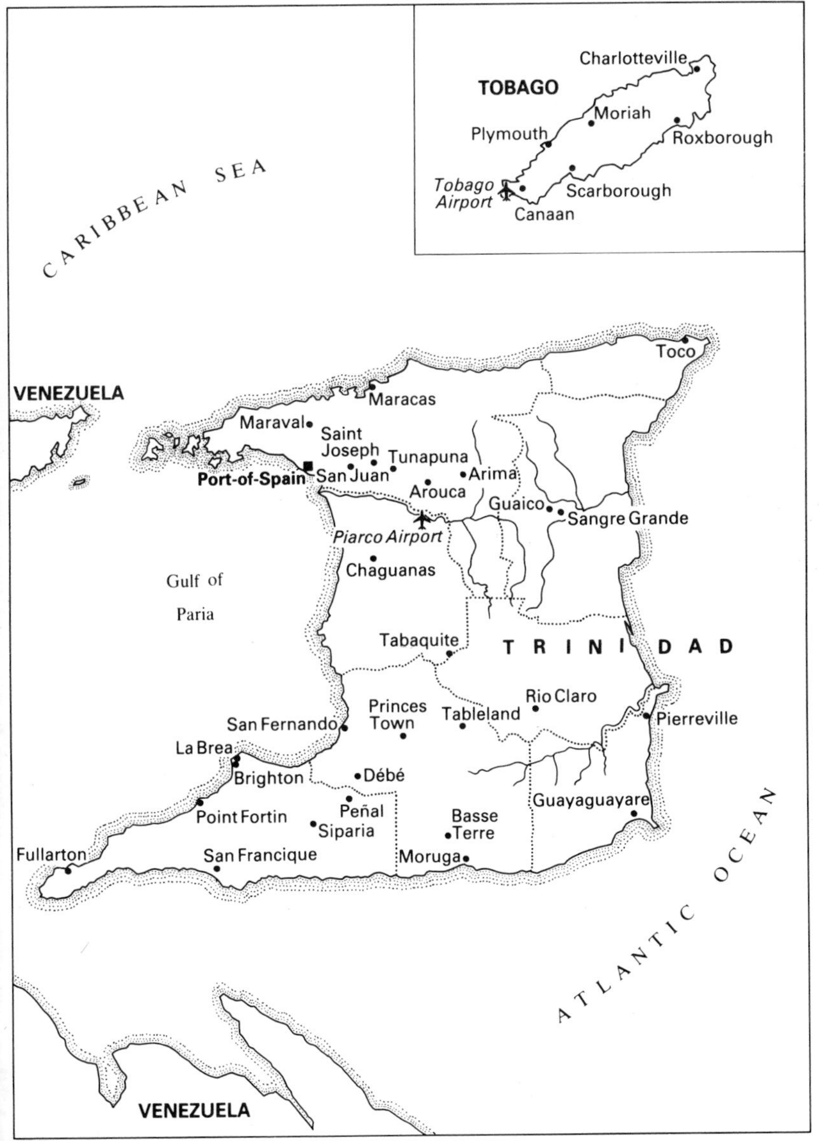